ecotone \ē′kə-tōn′\ n:

a transitional zone between two communities, containing the characteristic species of each; a place of danger or opportunity; a testing ground.

eco Greek oik-os, house, dwelling + *tone* tonos, tension.

We are grateful for support from the following donors:

Michael Glancy
Friend

George & Carol de Gramont
Sponsors

Joan H. Gillings
Founding Benefactor

Diane Brann
Benefactor

Join the Friends of *Ecotone*

$5000 — **Founding Benefactor**
Lifetime subscription

$2000 — **Benefactor**
Five-year subscription

$1000 — **Patron**
Three-year subscription

$500 — **Sponsor**
Two-year subscription

$200 — **Friend**
One-year subscription

Donations are tax-deductible.

ECOTONE
reimagining place

VOLUME 2, NUMBER 2
SPRING 2007

editor-in-chief
DAVID GESSNER

advisory board
BARBARA BRANNON, MARK COX, PHILIP GERARD,
SARAH MESSER, ROBERT SIEGEL, MICHAEL WHITE

managing editor
JAY VARNER

associate editor
MIRIAM PARKER

editors
LAUREN BREEDEN HODGES, nonfiction
CHRIS MALPASS, poetry
SUMANTH PRABHAKER, fiction
LINDSEY RONFELDT, poetry
HILLARY WENTWORTH, nonfiction

designer
SUMANTH PRABHAKER

copyeditors
JENNIFER CARLYLE
HILLARY WENTWORTH
DOUGLASS BOURNE

editorial staff
PAT BJORKLUND, DOUGLASS BOURNE, JENNIFER CARLYLE,
KRISTIN COLE, DAVID HOWELL, ASHLEY HUDSON,
KERRY MOLESSA, HEATHER NICHOLS, ADAM PETRY,
MELISSA ROBON, RACHEL RYAN, JENNIFER SHEPARD,
MEGAN SHEPHERD

Ecotone: reimagining place (ISSN 1553-1775) is published twice yearly by the Department of Creative Writing and the Publishing Laboratory at the University of North Carolina Wilmington. We are grateful for funding from the Landfall Foundation and the UNCW Department of Creative Writing. Subscriptions: $15 (one year, two issues). Single copies and institutional subscriptions are also available.

Please address all correspondence to *Ecotone: reimagining place*, Department of Creative Writing, University of North Carolina Wilmington, 601 S. College Road, Wilmington, NC 28403-3297 For submission guidelines, please consult page 189, or visit us online at www.uncw.edu/ecotone.

Copyright © 2007 by the University of North Carolina Wilmington.

On the cover: *Bubble Wish Face*, 2003, Anthony Goicolea. Graphite, ink, colored pencil, and ink on vellum and Plexiglas, 30" x 42".
On the back: *Starry Night*, 2004, Anthony Goicolea. Graphite, acrylic, and ink on Mylar with plexi glass, 36" x 43".

Paintings by Anthony Goicolea appearing on pages 61–68:
Disassembly, 2006. Graphite, ink, and acrylic on Mylar, 65" x 42".
Balseros, 2005. Graphite, ink and acrylic on Mylar, 36" x 53".
Constellation, 2006. Graphite, ink, and acrylic on Mylar, 24" x 19".
Cat's Cradle, 2004. Acrylic, ink, and graphite on Mylar in Plexiglas frame, 24" x 79".
Petroleum Dream, 2006. Graphite, ink, and acrylic on Mylar, 92" x 144".
Red Sky, 2005. Acrylic, ink, and graphite on Mylar in Plexiglas frame, 60" x 84".
Bloodstone, 2005. Acrylic, ink, and graphite on Mylar in Plexiglas frame, 36" x 56".
All images © Anthony Goicolea.

ISBN 978-0-9791403-0-3
Printed in U.S.A. at Thomson-Shore, Inc., Dexter, Michigan

Contents

From the Editor   On Space   vii

creative nonfiction

Susan Zakin	Men in the Dunes	1
Christopher Cokinos	The Dictionary as Field Guide	35
Brandon R. Schrand	Eleven Ways to Consider Air	70
Tenaya Darlington	Whole Hog	94
Sarajane Woolf	Auto Parts	108
Terry Marshall	By Canoe Into My Father's War	126
Jacqueline Kolosov	Along the Camino de Santiago	145
Emily Moore	Red Right Returning	159

fiction

Karen E. Bender	Candidate	10
Ray Morrison	Cityscape	26
Luanne diBernardo	No Motive	88
Elizabeth Crane	Varieties of Loudness in Chicago	100
Ron Savage	A Near Life Experience	118
Katie Rose Guest	Guantanamera	144
Jonatha Ceely	The Pond	155

poetry

Bob Hicok	Morphology, or the study of morphing	9
	Some of My Intimates	106
Dan Albergotti	Day Eight	25
	A Prayer for My Daughter, Who Does Not Exist	154
Tony Hoagland	Vaguely Listening to Something in Italian Played through an Intercom	46
	Noon	48
Maya Jewell Zeller	Socioeconomic	69
Gabrielle Jesiolowski	ohio from the fleeting	83
William Reichaed	Kinderszenen	84
Jean Esteve	Across the Street	93

maps

Clyde Edgerton	Three Maps	50
Rick Moody	Three Maps	123

the ecotone interview

with Bill McKibben	54

art

Anthony Goicolea	Eight Drawings	60

notes on contributors

183

On Space
From the Editor

About six years ago I became friends with the great nature writer John Hay and that friendship has been a source of deep pleasure for me. One day, while I was visiting him in Maine, we found ourselves talking about his near-contemporary, Rachel Carson.

"She had a place just down the road in Boothbay," he said. "That house was her salvation when the world attacked her."

He shook his head.

"The things they did to that woman were criminal. After she wrote that wonderful book she got so attacked and insulted by the goddamn money people, by the chemical companies and all. They called her a communist and pervert. The poor woman was dying of cancer at the time. They killed her before she died."

In a time when our government sneers at the science of global warming and evolution, it's worth remembering the bravery of the dying Carson in the face of that ugly slander. But this morning as I walked the beach near my house I thought about John's comments in a different light, with an emphasis not on the political savagery that Carson endured, but on the solace she found in her coastal home, her place away from the world, where she could focus on tidal pools and hermit crabs, on art and science. With the centennial of Carson's birth upon us we will likely be hearing a lot about the changes that *Silent Spring* wrought; namely the banning of DDT and other chemicals, and the return of many threatened species as a result. But what interests me just as much as those changes is where they came from, how the most public of effects began in the most private of places. It was within her retreat on those Maine beaches, deep in her own thoughts and in her own place, that Carson began to develop the insights and thoughts that would so impact the world. And it seems to me that in this way Rachel Carson epitomizes the way so many writers, and scientists, find their lives pulsing between retreat from and engagement with the world. In fact, because of the way that Carson moved between an intensely private life—full of contemplation and quiet observation—and a political life with worldly consequences, she seems an almost archetypal example of a central contradiction of the writing life. To some extent, we are all worldly hermits.

Before he retired to Maine, John Hay lived in a modest house atop a hill on Cape Cod, the house surrounded by many acres of scrub oak. "It's like a fortress up there with the winding road and the hill," a friend of John's said to me before I visited. "He's got a buffer from all the busyness. I'm surprised he hasn't built a moat."

During my first visit with John, he addressed his need for that buffer.

"Why did I come here to the middle of nowhere?" he said. "What was I looking for? I suppose I came here following some vague urge for space. You have to understand that when I was a boy the population of this country was only about ninety million—now there are three hundred and twenty million of us! This town had only eight hundred people, a small village. I suppose I had a hunch that it was space that I was after in coming here."

Space was one of the key words in John's vocabulary, a hieroglyph that held the key to many of the choices he had made in his life. It took me a while to begin to understand what he meant by the word. During our early meetings it seemed somewhat vague and nondescript. It was only later that I would begin to see that it was synonymous with freedom. And I would begin to see that it was also connected, in ways I wasn't quite sure of yet, to creativity and wildness.

Another writer who retreated in New England had a different way of putting the same thing. Melville spoke of the need for writers to be at least part recluses—or, in his term, "isolatoes"—and he believed in putting up walls to build the atmosphere necessary for the most intense sort of creation. Exhibit A would be the final draft of *Moby Dick*, written far from the sea in western Massachusetts, with Melville staring out his window at the whale of Mount Greylock. He wrote all day, sinking himself into his "strange wild work," while drinking six cups of tea until a perceptible halo of moisture arose from his head. It is a romantic picture, but it reveals a practical truth: that one of the conditions necessary for great and intense writing may be something as simple as space.

From the Editor

Over the past few years, I've given myself a reading list of isolatoes: Montaigne in his study within his chateau, quotes of old Greeks and Romans engraved in the thick wood beams; E. B. White in his spartan boathouse with the window framing Penobscot Bay; Robinson Jeffers up in the Hawk Tower, built out of stone with his own hands, beside Tor House, also hand-built, staring out at the Pacific from his cliff at Big Sur; And yes—why not?—the king of the clichés of retreat, Henry David Thoreau in his cabin at Walden. All of these writers argued for the artists' need to escape from the world. Montaigne wrote, "We must reserve a back shop all our own, entirely free, in which to establish our real liberty and our principal retreat and solitude." E. B. White seconded the motion in describing his boathouse: "It is because I am semidetached while here that I find it possible to transact this private business with the fewest obstacles."

I admit that it is a strange and contrary impulse to focus on retreat during times of war, when you can't help but find a military connotation in the word. But one thing I've learned from my reading is that retreat often leads to its opposite. For instance, in 1937, a decade before John Hay's move to Cape Cod, E. B. White, then 38, left New York City behind and headed up to his farm in Maine. In Barbara Mallonee's beautiful essay "Reading E. B. White: Perfect Pitch, Perfect Catch," I found White's own description of his move: "A person afflicted with poetic longings of one sort or another searches for a kind of intellectual and spiritual privacy in which to indulge his strange excesses." But one odd byproduct of this retreat, starting about the time of Hitler's first advancements, was that White's "determinedly personal essays," to use Mallonee's term, became increasingly, though subtly, political: suddenly within those essays sentences about the war began intertwining with those about chickens.

In this turn to the political he was not alone among my gallery of retreaters. All of these supposed recluses were, strange as it might sound, determinedly political—Thoreau most obviously and famously, with the ripples he caused in Walden Pond spreading outward to, among other places, India and the American South, with both Ghandi and Martin Luther King Jr. acknowledging Thoreau as a main, if not *the* main, influence on their work. Then there's Montaigne, emerging from his retreat to work as a prominent political advisor during the French civil wars, and Jeffers, who went from literary superstar to pariah because he stuck to his larger biocentric view of the world, a view forged in the privacy of his wanderings in Big Sur, and because he vehemently opposed World War II, even as his country swelled with patriotism.

And finally there's Rachel Carson, who by closely observing her tidal pools and eel grass, gave us a book that led to the most lasting environmental changes of the last century. One ecotone we have tried to inhabit in this journal is between literature and the politics of environmentalism, and it seems to me that one could do worse than take Carson as a model, both as artist and activist. During these crowded times, with the world warming and the concept of space under assault as population soars and privacy disappears, we need to remember to occasionally put the cell phone down and turn off the computer, and retreat into our own back shops or boathouses. Like the other members of my gallery of isolatoes, Rachel Carson reminds us of the necessity of retreat, and puts the lie to the more cowardly definitions of the word. She shows us that by continuing to return to our most private places, we are deeply engaging the world.

reimagining place
ECOTONE

VOLUME 2, NUMBER 2
SPRING 2007

Men in the Dunes
SUSAN ZAKIN

"We're the bad people who are ruining the earth."
 I smile. He smiles. He looks like Sam Peckinpah, road-worn and grizzled. His friend is younger, a Brad Pitt look-alike stalled out somewhere east of Hollywood. The Southern California desert always reminds me of Charlie Manson, and I am alone with two unshaven stragglers from the annual orgy of off-road vehicle recreation in the Algodones Dunes, one hundred miles southeast of Palm Springs. Dunes, these dunes, any dunes, have a look of eternity about them. They mark time, moving in the wind, yet their spareness evokes timelessness. Dust to dust, one recalls, seeing the way sand dunes reach for—yet never quite—touch the horizon.
 In our time the Algodones Dunes have been notable for this simultaneous evocation of the eternal and the immediate. Perhaps it's the proximity to Los Angeles that makes the elevated and the profane rub up against each other in such a casual, postmodern way: the campy sci-fi movie *StarGate* was filmed here, using the dunes as a backdrop for Egypt in 8,000 BC, when a malevolent alien took over the body of a young boy who might easily have been mistaken for Isaac Mizrahi's assistant during Fashion Week. ("Give my regards to King Tut, asshole!" was one of the film's more memorable lines.)
 Well, this is America. Eternity is a mass-market enterprise. Off-road vehicle enthusiasts flock to the dunes on winter weekends and holidays. One Thanksgiving weekend saw a veritable pupu platter of violent crime among off-roaders: one murder, two stabbings, two fatal accidents, and in the words of a *New York Times* reporter "innumerable brawls."
 I have driven out here on the advice of an environmental lawyer who told me that this lookout point is a good place to see the damage done by off-road vehicles: this is the line between the protected wilderness and the degraded landscape, pristine and debauched nature. But

I'm not concentrating on the view. I'm wondering if I'm going to be raped and killed.

"What do you guys do for a living?" I ask heartily.

"We're safecrackers," says Sam Peckinpah.

The younger man nods solemnly.

The older man hands me a business card. He explains that he—Dave Beck—and the younger man, whose name is Kidd, David Kidd, reclaim safes that have been abandoned. The card is reassuring, although I'm not entirely convinced. I comfort myself by thinking that if they are safecrackers, at least they're professional enough to have a business card.

"Have a seat," the older Dave offers. I hesitate and again the thought occurs that I'm about eighty miles from anyone who might hear me if I scream. I wonder why I was less nervous interviewing a suspected murderer when I was a reporter just out of college. I guess it's the isolation of this promontory, the undulating desert. The silence.

"Thanks," I say, plopping myself in a plastic lawn chair.

"So what's the appeal?" I ask, pointing at the all-terrain vehicles parked near the RV. I never saw any socially redeeming value to all-terrain vehicles, or ATVs—and if there is hedonistic value, it's lost on me. They're loud, they stink, and they're kind of stupid-looking. But, hey, maybe I'm missing something.

The guys tell me about the high-end stuff, how expensive the whole scene can get. A loaded ATV can cost sixty thousand dollars. It's the desert white-trash equivalent of a Donzi, the *Miami Vice*–ish speedboat, and this is a sea made of fractured bits of land. The men tell me that other parts of California have become more restrictive, so they've come out here, the last frontier.

The desert and the ocean are refuges for people who don't like authority. I count myself in that group, and, in a peculiar way, I feel sympathetic to these guys. *Whose side are you on?* I ask myself, not for the first time. Temperamentally, I sometimes find myself more comfortable with the bad guys. They have appetites.

Appetites, as any adult has learned, are destructive, perhaps inevitably so. That's certainly true here. The Algodones Dunes, one thousand square miles of scalloped peaks and ridges made of old lake sediments, are not only a mecca for rowdy SoCal white trash, but a place where unusual configurations of plants and animals have evolved to hang on to land that has all the stability of a Surrealist painting. The Pierson's milk vetch, for example, has the distinction of being the first plant placed on the federal threatened species list during the Bush administration. (One may well ask if it was the only plant placed on the endangered list during this notoriously anti-environmental presidency. But that would be too easy.) After environmentalists threatened to sue because the milk vetch, among other plants and animals, was getting smashed under the wheels of ATVs, the US Bureau of Land Management signed a temporary agreement placing almost fifty thousand acres of dunes off-limits to motorheads. The Maginot Line is right in front of us. This contested border is what I've come to see, I tell the men.

Big Dave offers me a bottle of juice—not beer, to my surprise.

"It's right over there," he says, pointing.

On one side of the line, the dunes are cluttered with life. Sandfood, a water-filled plant prized by the early inhabitants of this region, grows in cartoonish clumps on the flanks of sand.

The dunes where people ride ATVs are just sand.

I realize that I like the bare dunes better. *Wrong, wrong, wrong. That is so wrong*, I think. *But, still. Just visually, in strictly aesthetic terms . . . .*

The dunes were bare in the Gran Desierto, the largest dune field in North America, when I had returned to them. Those dunes made by the Colorado River Delta glowed pink in the reflected light of sunset. I smile to myself at the memory of how I had refused to turn back until we had climbed the highest of the dunes. The sun, the exertion, the bare flanks of sand appeared to me as a hallucination. One thing those dunes did was erase time.

The English knew it first, those colonialists. Clock time, according to the British historian E. P. Thompson, created the arbitrary divisions of our lives that tore us away from nature, and ourselves. In *Lawrence of Arabia*, Peter O'Toole played a wonderfully peroxided T. E. Lawrence who goes native, robbing trains with an Arab warlord. In the film's climax, an American reporter snaps photographs of Lawrence walking along the tops of the freight cars with the stride of a god. The screen is filled by the motion of Lawrence's high leather boots.

Later, as Lawrence sits buffing the aforementioned boots, the reporter asks, "What is it, Major Lawrence, that attracts you personally to the desert?"

Lawrence looks up.

"It's *clean*," he says.

A moment later, Auda abu Tayi, the warlord played by Anthony Quinn, shows up with an enormous clock, crowing that he has made a good trade with another looter. He winds the clock, then holds it up to his ear. It doesn't work. He shakes it. Then he smashes it.

"I must find something honorable," he growls.

Clock time, industrial time, time of the mega-machine: not honorable. The desert is the antithesis of all that. I found something honorable, enveloped by the sun, walking without stopping in the dunes of the Gran Desierto.

Honesty compels me to admit I am not always quite so honorable. I crave the sublime whether it takes the form of sanctity or sin. Looking down from this paved promontory, I realize I don't care so much if a landscape is pure, like the winter dunes of Desierto, or impure, like these battered dunes. I just want the proper aesthetic. I wonder if the illusion of purity—O'Toole's peroxided hair—is as good or better than the actual thing. ("If you were any prettier, it would have been called *Florence of Arabia*," Noel Coward told O'Toole.)

"Are you one of those tree-huggers?" Dave asks.

Here we go again, I think. Debates between rednecks and tree-huggers in the American West tend to be repetitive and, quite frankly, dumb. Like many of my colleagues in journalism, I have reached a point where I can bear neither the manipulative self-righteousness of environmentalists ("Are you going to mention our group?" one asked me, when I call to ask about the dunes) nor the ignorant rants of those who feel threatened by them.

"Let me ask you a question," I say to Dave. "What if the environmentalists are right and you guys are messing up the dunes? What if you *are* killing the plants and the lizards?"

"That stuff grows back," he tells me. "They've already taken us off, what is it, Dave? Sixty thousand acres? A hundred thousand? We've got twelve thousand measly little acres here."

The buzzing sound of an ATV interrupts us. A man rides up, his ill-cut hair flying out behind him. Dan Conklin owns an off-road equipment and towing business in the nearby town of Glamis. Conklin, a high-cheekboned guy with deep-set eyes, broad shoulders, and an apparent lack of access to quality dentistry, grew up in San Diego but now he lives in this desert outpost with its locked-down windswept buildings. To the newspaper-reading public, Glamis is a byword for Ecstasy and cocaine-fueled redneck bashes. For Conklin, Glamis is a chance to find himself. The forty-two-year-old former trucking company worker rescues the rowdy ATVers when they get stuck in the sand, a common occurrence.

"It's a small gold mine," he says. "I've made more money in the last six months than I made in San Diego in an above-average job. My family has some money, but I wanted to do it on my own. They respect me for it."

The American dream. The season at Glamis lasts only six months but Conklin tells me that he sticks around in the summer to protect his investment. Probably he's just gotten used to living out here. There is no electricity and no potable water in Glamis, where the water table is polluted by cyanide from an actual gold mine. But in the summer evenings Conklin has the dunes to himself.

"I just come out here and think. Watch the sun go down," he says.

Conklin doesn't believe he hurts the dunes. None of them do.

They're wrong. These ATVs kill plants and animals, especially when a quarter of a million of them descend on the desert. It's been documented that ATVs kill desert tortoises, which are endangered here in the Mojave. Kangaroo rats go deaf from the engine noise. There doesn't seem to be anyplace that can withstand these things, unless it's already bereft of life. In a Virginia wildlife refuge, off road vehicles have decimated ghost crab populations, wiped out thousands of sanderlings, and compacted sand so that sea turtles could no longer nest.

In an hour of walking the dunes I've seen three flattened, dried-out lizards, crushed by tires. Flat-tailed horned lizards, common here but rare enough to be candidates for federal protection, burrow under the sand to stay out of the heat. These guys wouldn't see the lizards even if they were looking for them. Which, of course, they're not. Besides, ATVs are so obnoxiously noisy and polluting that my cousin, a sensible gray-haired former science editor in her seventies, tells me she fantasizes about taking them out with a sniper rifle. If she takes out one of the riders by mistake, well, let God sort 'em out, is her attitude.

I don't mention any of this. The men gossip about the last big gathering, which took place on New Year's Eve. My attention wanders until I hear the word rape. I stop breathing and I only start again when I realize they're talking about a seamy murder case that's been in the newspapers and on TV. A man abducted a little girl and killed her. He was in this parking lot, just a few months ago. The little girl was here, too, locked inside his camper, presumably still alive.

Conklin says he towed this guy's vehicle when it became stuck in the deep sand.

"They said he burned her body." Conklin shakes his head. "He had all this wood with plastic wrap around it outside his RV."

"Do you think she was in there?" I ask.

"I know she was."

We are quiet. Conklin stares out at the sand.

Conklin makes a living getting people out of trouble. He also makes a living helping people destroy plants and animals. This is the paradox of environmentalism: we struggle against the inconsistency of our own nature. Human nature. That's the real reason we lose.

I try to understand these men. I'd rarely felt this rush from a machine, but I know it's possible. I had recently stopped seeing a Yale-educated emergency room doctor, a perfectly respectable National Public Radio–listening soccer dad, who, like Conklin, made a living getting people out of trouble, people with every kind of trouble you can imagine. He was also an adrenaline junkie and he loved cars. Among his many vehicles was an M3. When I mention this car to men I rarely have to add the acronym "BMW" or the description "rally car"—they know what it is. Driving the M3 made me realize why middle-aged men, and middle-aged women, buy hot cars. Taking the car just short of a skid on the rainy streets of suburban Sacramento one night, I felt an excitement I hadn't felt since I drove stick for the first time at nineteen with a head full of coke and a big-city reporter trying to kiss me every time I slammed it into neutral.

Was my doctor different from these men in the dunes? Was I? The doctor had grown up on the other side of the class divide; he wouldn't ride an ATV on the dunes, of course. Yet I had watched him inflict pain, in large part because of his unwillingness to confront pain directly, whether the pain of others or his own. He possessed a subterranean anger of impressive proportions. Attempts to expunge our destructive tendencies seem doomed to failure. I've come to believe that the will to destroy is not only ineradicable but can actually allied to the desire to protect, and with the right trigger, they feed each other. Over time, destruction is likely to win, if only because it has the power to erode what lies in its path, while protection only maintains the status quo. I understand the impulse to destroy, at least with destruction something *happens*.

These dunes will be opened and closed, fought over, treasured and marred. In the end, only fragments will remain.

I may have given up on environmentalism. Tucson, the place I once loved, a pottery shard of Mexico broken off from the mainland, a separate world where the desert informed every beat of life, is nothing special anymore, just another bastion of dull vulgarity and suburban sprawl. Recently, I'd found myself taking comfort from mundane things I once would have considered pathetic: a saguaro cactus at the side of a suburban street, the sound of rain, children running outside a house. I wonder if moments of grace are all I have left. I once felt intensely alive. What happened in the meantime?

Was I trying to find purity in the desert? Again? In Southern California, of all places? Did I expect it to be *clean?* It ain't the movies, sister.

"Sun's over the yardarm," I tell the men. "I better go."

"I bet you've never been on one of these," says grizzled Sam Peckinpah–Big Dave, nodding toward the ATV parked in the sun.

"It's not my kind of thing," I say.

"How can you write about something if you've never tried it?" Big Dave challenges.

"If I tried everything I wrote about, I'd be dead." I smile. One of my standard lines.

"It won't kill you," Dan Conklin says. He looks at me pleadingly, and I can't refuse the vulnerability I see in his face.

When I climb on behind him, Conklin delicately avoids pressing his body against mine. Any woman who has danced with a man, that is to say, every woman, will understand the subtlety I am describing. It's like this: In the Negev Desert I rode and then led a camel and, when I was leading, felt his muzzle at the back of my head although he never touched me, not once. This eight-foot-tall unwieldy beast never lost the breath of contact, yet at most, in nearly a quarter of a mile, he grazed the outer hairs of my head.

Conklin drives slowly, then winds it up as we climb a tall dune. When I squeak, he slows down. After a while I'm not squeaking.

"Gun it," I say.

"Did you say gun it?" he asks, looking back at me.

"Yeah," I tell him. "Go."

I take off the tinted goggles. I want to feel closer to the blistering white sand and the sky. The sky in the desert is deep and bright. There is nothing like it.

My mind is very clear but I am not in this place. I am remembering the Desierto. I was breathless, then, but in a different way. I followed the contours of the dunes: their flanks moving subtly under my weight, turning pages of sand as if the dunes were a novel that would never end. The sun held me. I heard the wind, knew the salt presence of the Sea of Cortez. Clock time stopped. I lost myself and found myself. Perhaps it was only chemical, the exertion of the climb producing endorphins of a higher quality than mere adrenaline.

Whatever it was, it felt *clean*.

"This is fun," I tell Conklin as we roll to a stop. "But it's not as much fun as walking."

"You don't like it," he says, and I feel terrible.

He looks crushed. I'm pretty sure Conklin doesn't meet too many women out here in the land of gearheads. What is more elemental, more natural, than small gestures of consideration between men and women, cease-fires in our unending war? There is clean, and there is ordinary life. Negotiating between the two may be the real work. Perhaps it is the only work. Or must we choose sides?

Small kindnesses ennoble us even as they soil us with compromise and mendacity. I choose. I am a collaborator, an appeaser, a Neville Chamberlin of the desert. I'll never be as beautiful or as blond as Peter O'Toole. Worse. I will be a suburbanite, because, face to face with this lonely man, who is not a bad man, after all, and whose loneliness I understand more than I care to admit, I cannot hurt him.

"It's fun," I say. "Really." I look at him with my sweetest, most girlish expression. I am protesting too much, forcing him to pretend he believes me, because I cannot bear to look upon his unhappiness, and, despite my good intentions, perhaps I am doing violence, of a sort, even as I insist on being kind. "Really," I say again, "I like it."

Morphology, or the study of morphing
Bob Hicok

I tend to brush my teeth right before I go to work.
When I don't, there's this space right before
I go to work into which other things
or nothing can creep. I've been reading a book
about rocks in the teeth brushing space,
which took the place of the washing my coffee cup
space, which I now leave unwashed, which is why
I stopped drinking coffee. I knew a guy
who believed we could do anything we set our minds to.
I asked him to be a guy who didn't believe that.
When he couldn't, I said check mate and we went for pizza
by the river. I need to stop writing
about wanting to change. My desire to change
is unchanging. But wanting to stop writing about change
is a desire to change. Sometimes it feels
like I'm both the prisoner and the warden in a movie
about a guy who didn't do it. How does the warden
escape being sadistic, given that the script calls
for sadism, how does the prisoner get more
of the rice pudding? If I ran a prison,
I'd make everyone wear corduroy pants
so their escapes would sound funny.
That would be different, like whimpering
feels transitional between crying all the time
and not crying all the time. This may be insensitive,
but do you ever feel like the wagons of your thoughts
have circled and you're inside, being shot at?
And you're rooting for those doing the shooting?
I won't ever notice all the things I never notice.
This is like saying something else
that means the same thing put a slightly different way.

Candidate
Karen E. Bender

It was four thirty in the afternoon, and Diane Bernstein knew that the phone was about to ring. She had just paid the babysitter, the third one to quit this month, extremely polite when she quit, blaming it on other issues—sorority functions, heavy schoolwork—as though the boy had not unnerved her at all. When Diane had walked through the door, Liza, the baby girl, fell into her mother's arms, weeping so hard she began to choke. The boy, Johnny, was curled up in his bed, rocking himself, for he had scratched the babysitter in a fury ("I had wanted to play the radio," she said, "and he just went insane") and the young woman had shut him in his room. Why hadn't Diane found a better babysitter? It was not a question she allowed herself anymore. She had long stopped worrying about forgiveness, of herself or others. When the therapist had told her, again, that it was not her fault, she laughed; everything was her fault; everything was everyone's fault. "Even if it was his fault," she said, meaning her husband, to the therapist, "What would it matter? He's gone."

Diane had to figure out who to comfort first: the two-year-old, Liza, who clung to her, frantic with love, unwilling to peel herself from her mother after their long day apart, or Johnny, curled up, a knot of frustration in his bed. "They're cute kids," the babysitter called back, apologetically, pulling her long sleeves over the scratches the boy had given her; clutching her fifty dollars, she got into her Jeep and drove off.

Diane had spent the day working in the remedial writing lab of a private university in the Southeast. She hunched in a dimly lit cubicle with the undergraduates, glossy, overfed children who drove SUVs that were gifts from their parents and who could not correctly use a comma. Their essays were supposed to address the presidential election, and involved passionate, ungrammatical declarations stating why the Republicans should win. *Lazy people should not get my tax mony*, they wrote, or *I dont want any gay agenda on my family. Marriage is between a man and a woman.* That day, Diane sat with a young woman dressed like a prostitute, her pink Spandex halter top stretched across her breasts. Her hair was styled in two pigtail braids. The girl smelled of the beach, of coconut and salt. She had written a diatribe about how the United States should not only take over Iraq but Saudi Arabia, Egypt, Russia, and Japan, as revenge for Pearl Harbor. It was an extremely long and angry run-on sentence.

"Do you worry about how other countries might respond to this?" asked Diane.

The girl glared at her. "The terrorists want to kill me," she said.

The girl's previous paper had recorded her frustrations about her parents' divorce, the insensitivities of her superiors at Wal-Mart, the cheap gifts her boyfriend had given her. It had been a more interesting paper, though it still lacked consistent punctuation.

"The terrorists would come to Briar Wood College?" Diane asked, before she could stop herself.

The girl's eyes narrowed. Then, as though concerned about her grade, she smiled and said sweetly, "You're just from the North," she said, which was true, though "the North" seemed to imply anywhere slanting north or west; Diane had moved here from Seattle.

Diane closed her eyes; the school where she worked had raised tuition too many times, and faculty had been cautioned not to discuss the election with the conservative students. They lurched about campus, students and teachers, ignoring each other's pins and T-shirts. She had done what she could: covered her car in bumper stickers and stuck yard signs in her lawn that were later torn down.

Now, at home, Diane thought it was best to unplug the phone. Then she would not have to decide whether to answer it. The father, who was now residing in Florida, was not supposed to call at this hour; he was supposed to only speak to the children in the morning, for his voice upset them when it was time for dinner and bed. She carried the girl up to the boy's room and sat on his bed. The children both fell upon her. Liza put her head on Diane's leg and closed her eyes, quiet; her breathing became calm. The boy did not like to be touched, but was generally soothed by coloring in squares in black and yellow. She gave him crayons and paper and he sat up, filling each box in with extraordinary love.

Diane listened to the silence in the room and envied the girl's belief that she had been rescued. It was an acute misunderstanding between parents and children, one which sometimes comforted her, but also felt like a joke. She sat in her son's bedroom and was overcome by loneliness so crushing it was hard to breathe. Her girl's tiny hands fumbled to grab her mother's waistband, and Diane was still as the girl gripped her, as though Diane was waiting to be pulled to a safe place.

Someone was knocking at the door. Diane jumped up, holding Liza, and she and Johnny ran to the door. She opened the door and found a man in a crisp white shirt and navy pants standing on the other side of it. He held out his hand as though slicing the air in two.

"Hi there," he said "Woody Wilson here. Running for state legislature. I want to represent you."

Before he said his name, he was just an ordinary stranger, standing there, slim, brown-haired—a salesman of encyclopedias or cleaning equipment—with the belligerent, trudging optimism of someone who went door to door. After he declared his name, she hated him. This shift in feeling was so abrupt that her heart felt like an emptied balloon. His face seemed to glow the way a famous person's did, as though it was an accident that he was walking around on earth. He lived most fully on the newspaper ads and billboards all over town. *Woody Wilson, Republican for North Carolina State Senate.*

"And what's your name?"

"Diane," said the boy.

"Man," the girl said, looking up at Woody Wilson.

It was late afternoon. The house smelled like a rotten melon. The afternoon was weighted toward night. The golden light already held an undertone of darkness. Diane had read what he stood for and she hated all of it. It would be so simple, so luxurious to slam the door on him! But she did not. His eyes were clear and blue as a baby's. Her heart began to march as though she had been waiting for him.

"Diane, can I have just a moment of your time?" he asked. He kept smiling, but his face was red from the heat. "I can see you're a family person." He stepped back and began to arrange the plastic vehicles scattered across her front porch. He put Big Wheel behind sedan. "I have a family, too. How old are your kids? I have two, eight years old and five." He laughed, brokenly; it almost sounded as though he was weeping. "I've come to ask for your vote, Diane," he said. "I am for family. We are what make America great." He swept his arm toward her in a grand, appropriating gesture; she stepped back from him. "What does your family need? If you want more money in your wallet, I have the answers. If you want better schools, I can answer that, too."

She tightened her arm around Liza's waist. She knew that her ideas were opposite to his in everything that made up a political belief. "And how are you going to make the schools better?" she asked.

He heard the blade in her voice; his eyes narrowed. The pale, clapboard houses behind him seemed to be melting in the heat. "Good question, Diane," he said, speaking quickly. "We want to bring faith back to our schools. Every child should be allowed to pray. No cost to the taxpayer." His words sounded a little breathless.

"Pray to what?" she asked.

He blinked. "I'd say Jesus," he said. She was silent. "But it's a free country," he said. He sounded hesitant on that one, she thought. He tapped a rolled-up leaflet against his hand.

"I believe in separation of church and state," she said, crisply.

He nodded vigorously, as though by making this movement they would be in agreement. The optimism in the gesture was ridiculous, almost moving. But then he handed her a leaflet. "Some folks may say it's hard to know whether to choose me or my opponent, Judy Hollis. So I wanted you to know this."

Did you know that JUDY HOLLIS is a lesbian?
That she is bringing her gay agenda to Raleigh?
Vote for WOODY. FAMILY VALUES.

She looked at the ad and her heart began to pound faster. She had seen it earlier that day, in the local newspaper. She set the baby down; she'd heard enough of the hate masquerading as more congenial agendas.

"Diane, our campaign is getting the word out," he said. "Judy is bad news for our state."

"Because she's gay?" she asked.

"Yes," he said. "We don't want them coming here. I stand for values, Diane, family values. You know what I mean—"

"No, I don't," she said. "I don't want to hear this bullshit. Just stop."

Woody blinked but did not move. The boy glared at Woody Wilson as though he were an animal the boy wanted to eat. He regarded most men who were tall with brown hair this way—it was the simplest way they could describe their father. The boy lay on the floor and rolled from side to side. Why did they work, the ways he tried to comfort himself? He rolled and screeched and turned; they were strategies which adults found amusing at two but now made them look away. The girl gazed at him. The girl's love for the boy poured out of her; she could not help herself. She stretched herself on top of him. She screeched and tried to lick his lips. "Stop!" the boy roared, trying to push her off. She clutched his foot as he tried to crawl away from her. Diane plucked the girl off the boy and set her on the couch, where the girl began to scream.

"Please," Woody Wilson said, "Let me say—" His face went white. Then he toppled forward onto her living room floor.

The girl let out a piercing shriek of delight, as though the man was entertaining them. The boy jumped back, his hands pressing his ears. "Stop!" he bellowed. He rolled into a ball on the floor.

Woody was lying face-down across Diane's hardwood floor. He seemed as incongruous as a whale washed up on a beach; she looked down at him, afraid. Diane lightly tapped his shoulder, then she rolled him over. His shoulder was soft as an avocado. He had recently had a breath mint and his breath was medicinal.

"What'd he do?" yelled the boy.

She jumped up and grabbed the phone off a side table. Woody's eyes opened, and he was staring at them.

"I'm calling a doctor," she said.

"Don't call anyone I don't want them to know." His presence on billboards made the mundane facts of his humanity strange and troubling. His forehead was pink, with creases in it like clay. There was golden hair on the backs of his hands. He touched his eyebrow; a dark bruise was forming. She was afraid of him, which translated into a great and useless pity. She rarely pitied anyone but herself now, so that superiority was somewhat enjoyable.

She left the front door open. Moths flew in. Woody Wilson put a hand on his forehead. "Ow," he said. He took a deep breath. "Exhaustion. That's what the doctor said. Nothing wrong at all. He said if it happens, sit down for a few minutes, take some breaths, and keep going. I have to keep going."

"Okay," she said, reluctantly. She felt vaguely afraid of being blamed.

"I don't know what happened," he said. "But when I feel strongly about something, sometimes I see black. I feel my heart churning. Perhaps the Lord is telling me something. Ow," he said, softly.

What did he mean, the Lord told him things? She sat in her cubicle every day, convincing her students: Evidence. A clear and organized argument. Sometimes she heard herself ranting about evidence, concrete examples, and she felt herself sweating, pathetically, with her own zealotry. He rubbed the bruise on his forehead. She went to the kitchen and brought him an ice pack. He sat up and pressed it to his face.

"Why are you running for office?" she asked.

"He told me to do this. Woody Wilson. I will stand for values. Speak out. The town needs to know your name."

Through the open front door the clouds were knitting together in a searing, bright sky. She could see the houses on their lawns, each life parceled out into its plot of land, the determined, clipped order of flowers and shrubbery. There were two registered Democrats on her street that she knew of, and four Republicans. They went in and out of their houses, shaving their lawns, picking up their newspapers, remarking on the weather. They would all walk into the voting booths, educated and uneducated, intelligent and dumb, and their votes would be worth the same. They sat, diligently filling in bubbles on paper, and, she thought, because of the voters' impulsive, careless yearnings, wars started, debts soared, the land grew barren, and their great-grandchildren would starve.

The bump on Woody's head was growing larger and darker. It made Diane ashamed, as though it somehow implied something sinister about her. The phone began to ring. Her husband felt most lonely around dinnertime. He did not love them, but did not know who else to call.

"I'm sorry," said Woody Wilson. His right foot tapped on the floor like a rabbit's. "A minute. I'll be on my way." He paused. "Does it look very bad?" he asked.

"I don't know," she said. "Maybe you should keep the ice on it."

The phone rang ten times and then stopped.

"Thank you very much, Diane," he said. He tapped his fingers on the floor rapidly. "I'll just be here a second. I'm a person who does best when he's busy. No one can say I don't have plans."

"All right," she said. "While you're here, I just have one question," she said, suddenly breathless. "Why do you hate so many people? Why so intolerant? I just want to know."

"I do not hate them," he said. "Listen. I am trying to help them from leading lives of so much pain—"

"Why do you assume that people who are not like you are in pain?" she asked.

"I know a lot about pain," he said. "My momma died when I was eight," he said briskly. "My father had to work three jobs. He was always tired. He was so tired he fell asleep on elevators, between floors. I had to get a job working a paper route when I was a small boy. I worked hard. I worked my way up, the good days and the bad. Hard work and faith, that's what got me to college, law school, where I am today."

He recited his litany of pain solemnly, as though it were a prayer. Everyone was competitive in terms of their pain. Whose pain was the worst? Did it matter more that Woody's mother had died when he was young or that Diane's husband had left the family? Was a troubled, problematic child a worse pain than infertility? What about the fact that Diane's hours working as a remedial composition instructor had been cut in half, the sudden eczema that spread across her skin, how did that weigh in compared to diagnosis with cancer, losing your family in a war, fearing that you might not make love to another person again?

"You were lucky you succeeded," she said. "Some people don't."

"It was not luck," he said sternly. "It was faith. Let me tell you something. A few months ago, before I decided to run for office, I was waking up one morning and I swore I saw a pitbull rush toward the bed. It wanted to eat me. It had a huge, pink mouth. It had been waiting for years for me. It was probably a dream, but it looked real. I said 'Jesus' and it disappeared."

The boy noticed Woody's bag of buttons and stickers. He began, methodically, to take them out and count them. The phone rang again.

"Don't you need to answer that?" Woody asked.

How did anyone know the right way to live a life? Diane's husband, at forty-five, had begun to feel pains in his chest. The pains were nothing, the doctor said, but anxiety, but her husband felt, abruptly, the slow, inevitable closing of his own life. He had awakened one night, damp and trembling, after dreaming that Johnny had his hands around his throat. In the dream he had peeled his son's hands off his throat and risen up, free, into the sky. She had these feelings too, for she had had her own disappointments—it had not been her dream to berate undergraduates about commas, for one thing—but she was going along with what was given them, and when she tucked the children in she had not thought there was anything else to do. But suddenly her husband believed that their family was killing him. He was almost gleeful in this, a solution. He was a large, healthy man, but after this dream, he began visiting doctors, checking not only his heart, but his lungs, his kidneys, his skin. He said that something was dirty in his blood. No doctors found anything. He searched the Internet for remote adventures; he logged onto sites that described trips into mountains, forests, deserts barely developed by human hands. He said he wanted to go somewhere clean. His home office—he was a freelance reporter for a variety of computer magazines—was papered with posters of Tibet, mountains white, iridescent with snow.

This business had intensified shortly after the doctor had explained to Diane and her husband that testing had placed their son on the autism spectrum. The boy, he said, loved rules so intensely it could be difficult for him to get married or live with someone. He might be tormented in public school, so make sure to explain his issues to the teachers. He could receive therapy to help him understand when another person was happy or sad. On the bright side, the boy would be proficient at math.

After they had heard this, her husband asked her to drive the car home. She stared at the shiny, broad backs of the cars in front of them. His silence made her aggressively talkative.

"I don't know if he was the best guy," she said. "We could see someone else."

He sat, hunched, arms wrapped around himself as though he were freezing.

"Don't you have anything to say?" she asked sharply, in the tone she sometimes used, despite herself, with the children.

He glanced at the dashboard. "We're low on gas," he said.

The phone stopped ringing. She counted; this time it took twenty rings. Woody lowered the ice pack. "Someone wants to talk to you," he said.

"No," she said. "Actually, he doesn't."

The boy looked up. "There are fifty-eight Woody Wilson buttons in your bag," he said.

"Really?" said Woody. "There are, I think, 108 signs all over town. Yard signs, billboards. I drive around counting them. My wife, Tracy, helped me put up the signs. She did a good job. It was a good day for her." He pressed the ice pack to his head and closed his eyes. "I am her rock," he said. "I am her anchor in troubled water."

The hope in his face, his desire to be seen in this role, made her look away.

"You are your husband's rock," he said eagerly. "I can see it." He picked up the ice pack again. "My wife used to work in real estate," he said. "Did I tell you? She sold a house three blocks away." He paused. "She was very happy," he said. "We had wine and steaks at the Port House." He was staring at his shoe with the frozen gaze of someone banishing other thoughts from his head. Then he quickly looked at her. "And what kind of work does your husband do?"

"I don't really know anymore," she said.

She did not yet know how to answer this. Should she say he was dead? "He left six months ago," she said. Telling Woody was practice, she told herself. She hated other people's pity; their sympathy, she felt, was a way of flattering themselves. She tried to laugh, a hollow, cheerless sound—why? She did not want him to be afraid of her. She was certainly afraid of herself. "That was him on the phone."

"I'm sorry," he said

A month before her husband had left, she had told him that she was picking up some milk at the supermarket and had checked into a motel instead. It was a one-story chain motel with a small aqua pool, one she had often passed and wondered who frolicked inside there, and this time she put her own key in the door. She had no idea what she would do in the room, as she was not meeting anyone there, but she bought a bag of chips from the snack machine, walked into room twenty-seven, and sat on the bed. She ate each chip slowly, trying to make the bag last a while. The room whitened with light every few seconds from the passing cars. She undressed and looked at her naked body in the mirror over the dresser. She did not look much different than she had ten years before; that was before she had met her husband. The fact that she did not look different seemed absurd. She lay on the bed. She tried to imagine an alternative life that she could have, but her fantasies were surprisingly clichéd: tipping champagne glasses in a fancy restaurant in a hotel, floating on a gondola on golden water. Why did she think these things would give her the feelings she wanted? She lay in the dim room and understood that her longing would never end. She lay in the darkness for half an hour. Then she got dressed and went home.

"When I'm feeling troubled," said Woody, "I let Him in my heart. I put myself in the hands of the Lord."

"What does that even mean?" she said. "What hands? What are you talking about?"

"I call his name when I cannot take another step." He looked at her as though she would understand this. "Do you ever feel that, Diane? Who do you call when you cannot take another step?"

She called Dr. Dawson, a woman in her sixties, who had a doctorate in clinical psychology. They sat in a drab, spare room in a mirrored office building, and Diane talked for fifty minutes to this woman who had red hair that was stiff like a meringue. The woman laughed at her jokes, listened when she cried, was quiet when Diane yelled at her. Occasionally Dr. Dawson would tell Diane facts about herself, such as the fact that she had enjoyed math as a child, or her own desire to write erotic poetry; somehow, these facts were always disturbing. But Diane never wanted to leave that room when the hour was up, not even for what relief she had gained during that hour, but the mere hope of it.

"I call Dr. Dawson," she said.

"What does she say?" he asked.

"She tells me that I am not my parents," she said.

"Who else would you be?"

"I don't know," she said.

He laughed carefully. "Have you thought why you have not given God a chance to mend your heart—"

"I'm my own responsibility," she said. "Now I don't have to act out the failings of my own parents. I am responsible for my own future. I know I can rely on myself." What did all of this mean? Did it mean simply getting up in the morning, driving the boy to school, handing the daughter to the babysitter, making sure they all had enough to eat, sitting in her cubicle for the appointed number of hours, driving home? What was that? Did it mean she could make herself happy? "So your wife sells real estate," she said lightly.

"She did until a year ago," said Woody.

He put down the ice pack and stared at it. When he looked up, he stared through her, as though another person was simply a clear window to some better view. "She won't get out of bed. She stays there with the curtains shut. She says the light hurts her hair," he said.

She looked at Woody Wilson, the blazing whiteness of his shirt, the way his hair was parted very neatly in the middle. She imagined him standing in front of the mirror that morning while his wife lay silent in the dim bedroom, drawing his comb tenderly through his hair. "I'm sorry," she said. "It sounds hard."

"Hard," he said, and laughed, a sad laugh. "Life is hard. But you know, marriage is a sacred union."

"Fine," she said, thinking that this was what she resented most of all, the lack of specifics, the cheerful vagueness, "but, you know, I think that each person has to give something."

"I give her my devotion," he said, sitting up, excited, ready for a debate. "She does the best she can. I wake up in the morning and sometimes I look at her face, and I just want to know what she is thinking. I tell her she needs to go to church. God will help her." His face was naked, a boy's face, the pale, terrible lids of a child. "I want people to see that I'm trying. I want people to say that Woody Wilson was a good man."

A few weeks before her husband had left, Diane had heard him crying at odd moments: when he was in the bathroom shaving, when he was in the garage taking in the trash. His crying was soft, private, not meant for her or the children, and each time she came upon it she felt both wounded and enraged. He never wept with her but away from her, and she knew that this meant she was not supposed to comfort him. One night, during this time, she had woken up and made his lunch for him. In the dark kitchen, she had put a peanut butter sandwich, an apple, a string cheese, and a cookie in a brown bag and left it on the counter. The next day, he took the bag to work and when he came back, he said, "I took your lunch today. Sorry."

She was suddenly ashamed of her gesture. "I know you did," she said, and they were both more familiar in this, the feeling of deprivation, their quiet, growing anger toward each other. The next morning, when she had woken up, that same lunch was on the counter; he had made it for her. She had wept, and had begun to eat it slowly; after a few bites, she stopped. He would be leaving soon; they both knew this. She sat in the empty kitchen and wondered at the point of these gestures, their ultimate selfishness.

The phone was ringing again. Woody clapped his hands over his ears. The boy suddenly stood up and went into the kitchen. The girl wandered off to join him. There was the scream, "Stop!" by the girl followed by the boy yelling, "Give it!" and then the sound of a body falling in the kitchen. "Oh no," Diane said. She ran into the kitchen. She heard the candidate stepping behind her.

The boy had the girl pressed to the floor with his body. She was coughing. He was trying to unpeel her tiny closed fist. "Give it!" he growled.

"I want it!" screamed the girl.

"Get off her!" Diane yelled at the boy. She grabbed his thin shoulders and tried to shake him off, but the boy would not move. "Now!"

Diane imagined how Woody Wilson saw them, the disheveled middle-aged woman in the putrid kitchen, wrestling with the enraged son who was stronger than she was. Legislate against this, she thought. The girl opened her mouth to bite the boy's hand.

Woody grasped the boy's hands. "Let go of your sister," said Woody quietly.

"She stole it!" screamed the boy.

Woody held a hand out, as though to calm the air. "Now wait, everybody," he said. "Wait." He reached into his pocket to pull out a Woody Wilson sticker. "I'll trade you." He handed the girl his sticker. "Vote for me." The girl grabbed it. She was already possessed of a startling rage, as though she foresaw the difficulties her own beauty, her brother's rantings, and her father's fumblings would bring her. When the girl stared at someone, as she did at her brother, Diane saw how she would someday regard a lover, the assumption that the other would feed some endless hunger inside of her. She gazed at Diane with the same expression, and Diane whispered to her, ashamed before its vastness.

The boy broke away from the girl. Woody pressed the boy's sticker back into his outstretched hand. The boy turned away from him and hunched over his sticker. It had the green, smiling face of Shrek on it.

"Where'd you get this?" Woody asked the boy.

"At school. They called my name in the cafeteria," the boy said. "I heard my name. They said it like this: John. Nee. Bern. Steen. They chose me. They said I could go home. The lady gave me this when I walked out. She said hold this and go right to the car. I held it the whole way."

Diane remembered this from the day before, the first time she had picked up her son by car at school. The car riders waited for their mothers in the cafeteria, while their parents, in cars at the traffic circle, told their names to the pickup coordinators, who called their names on the walkie-talkie. "Johnny Bernstein," Diane had said to the coordinator. She imagined her son's name floating over the loudspeaker in the cafeteria, where the children were sitting on long steel benches. She pictured all the children. Johnny and Keesha and Juan and Christopher and Sandra and the others, hunched over the tables, waiting to be summoned back to their lives. How many times in their lives would they sit like this, waiting to be called—for work, for love, for good fortune or bad, for luck or despair? What joys or sorrows would each of them be chosen for? She wished she could see how her son hurried down the dingy, dim brown public school corridor, how he walked to the doors that burst open to the afternoon light.

She was relieved when she saw him coming to her car; it was as though he had just been born. "What happened?" she asked. He had told her the same thing: "They said my name like this." Her son cupped his hands together and spoke into them: "John. Nee. Bern. Steen." He said these words with awe, as though they had been spoken by the voice of God. She watched his face in the rearview mirror, blank but suffused with a new brightness, and she wanted to touch his young face and feel what hope was in it, but she simply drove on.

Now Woody leaned toward the boy. "John. Nee. Bern. Steen. You did a good job," Woody said.

The boy nodded at Woody's correct pronunciation. "Yes," he said.

"Your parents will be proud," Woody continued.

"My father calls in the morning," Johnny said. "I hear him, but I don't see his face."

"He must miss you," said Woody. Stop, she thought. Don't pity him. Woody rolled up his shirt sleeves. He bent so he was looking into the boy's face. "Johnny," said Woody, "I know how you feel. When I was a boy, I woke up and the house was quiet. No one called me. Johnny, I didn't have a mother. My father was at work long before I got up." He ran his hand through his hair. "I dressed and got myself to the bus stop. I rode the school bus. I waited for it to pick me up. Some days it took a long time. Sometimes I said my name, too. *Woody Wilson.* I said it over and over. *WoodyWilson.WoodyWilson.WoodyWilson.* There was a bar beside the bus stop. Sometimes a couple men would be sleeping in the doorway. They looked dead. They smelled terrible. Johnny, I said my name so many times it was like a prayer. *Woody Wilson,* I said, *you are not those men. You are yourself."*

His voice had become quieter as he spoke to Johnny. The boy gazed at him, strangely lulled. She felt the little girl grab her leg and Diane touched her hair. How many more moments would Woody speak to her son? And how had her life come to this, hoarding minutes of kindness doled to them by strangers who knocked on her door? She wondered if this would be the future texture of their lives, this hoarding, and she wished Woody Wilson would leave, but also appreciated the fact that someone else was in the room. She looked away from his pale, thin hair, his shirt rolled halfway up his pinkish arms. She was suddenly afraid that her son would ask him to stay.

But the boy suddenly turned his back to Woody, squatting over his stickers with a fierce expression. "Johnny?" Woody asked. "Are you all right?"

"I don't care," said the boy sharply. "Guess what? I don't care."

She did not know what would comfort him; she barely knew what would comfort herself.

"Well," said Woody. "Hey." His voice broke a little, and he laughed, a hearty, rehearsed laugh. "Well, you never know what will work with kids, what will help them. Never hurts to try, right, Diane? Got to keep trying?"

He touched his hair as though to check that it still existed, that he was all here. He wanted to be reassured, and so did she, and for what? They were soft, graying, halfway to their deaths. They both knew that no one could understand another person's love, parent or child's; they both knew that everyone would die alone.

"Okay," she said carefully, and shrugged.

"Thank you," he said.

The tinny sound of the "Star-Spangled Banner" burst into the room. It was Woody Wilson's cell phone. Woody's face assumed a stern expression as he held it to his ear. "Yes. Still on Greenfield. Yep." He turned it off. "Well," he said. "Time to go."

He picked up his briefcase. "Thank you for your hospitality, Diane," he said brightly. The politician's voice burst out of him as though he were on the radio; he seemed almost surprised to hear it. He smiled as he had in the billboard, holding out his hand. "Goodbye," he said.

"Goodbye," she said, shaking his hand, the firm, remote grip of a stranger. She felt his pulse jump in his hand and it startled her; she let go and stepped away.

Standing on Diane's front porch, Woody Wilson slipped his briefcase under his arm. The bump on his head was dark and monstrous. "What should I tell people?" he asked. "How did this happen?"

"I don't know," she said. "Tell them you tripped."

"Yes," he said, brightening, as though delighted by the idea of simplicity. "I just tripped."

Silence bore down on them; there was nothing more to say. Woody Wilson hurried up the sidewalk to the next house, lifting a hand to knock on the door. Outside, the sunlight was dying. His lips were moving; she believed that he was murmuring his name. She heard the phone begin to ring again. Quickly, she stepped out the door into the cooling, pink air. She looked at the names of all the candidates stuck into the green lawns. They sat, arranged in rows under the sky, fluttering in the low wind. She stood for a moment, reading the names displayed there; then she turned and went back into the house.

Day Eight
Dan Albergotti

The lord is embarrassed. He realizes
only now that he will have to inhabit
the world he has made. He will be made
to endure the praises of the thinking creatures
and the indifference of the beautiful ones.
It's going to be hell. It's going to be
day after day after day of regret and chagrin.
And he wishes he had not made the son
a sacrificial lamb. He wishes he had not
made the daughter's hair auburn.
He wishes he had not left so many questions.
He almost wants to apologize for the mosquito.
It's only morning, but it already feels
like a long day. He's already thinking about the rain.

Cityscape
RAY MORRISON

1.

One of the great charms of the mid-sized Southern city in which I live is the hodgepodge of neighborhoods that fill its borders, each unique and reflective of the people who live in them. One of the oldest, and largest, is an irregular grid of streets filled with closely packed single-family houses. This neighborhood bridges two large medical centers, and is home to a diverse group of doctors, teachers, students, and other upwardly mobile types, as well as working-class families. For decades, it enjoyed a reputation as a friendly, almost quaint neighborhood, well-known for lazy summer evenings idled away in front porch gatherings and temperate autumns when small children would run and play up and down the sidewalks.

Several years ago, during the week after Thanksgiving, a newly arrived family decorated their house for Christmas. The display was enormous and elaborate, with every bush and tree adjacent to the home ablaze with hundreds of colorful bulbs. The house, too, was framed with blinking lights. But the centerpiece of the holiday display was an enormous nativity scene set up across the front lawn. The figures of the crèche were life-sized and included the three Magi and several animals. The owners had also carefully wired an angel to the eave so it hung suspended above the scene, as large as any of the figures below it, its wings and arms spread wide. The angel was positioned below a large, illuminated star fastened atop the roof.

The display quickly became the talk of the neighborhood and even found itself the subject of stories in the newspaper and on the local TV news. Following the appearance of these stories, people from all over the city, county, and beyond began driving by to witness it, necessitating that the family keep the display lit up later and later each night to accommodate the viewers.

But as it turned out, the great, bright star that shone down on the holy scene was situated on the roof such that it was exactly even with the window to the neighbor's master bedroom. So bright was this star that, even with the blinds closed, its brightness punched through enough to light the room as though it were midday. The couple who lived in this neighboring house, a middle-aged insurance executive and his wife, explained the problem to the newcomers, making it clear that they weren't angry, certain that the people with the ornate decorations would be embarrassed when they learned of their unintended rudeness.

It turned out the new arrivals were devout fundamentalists who informed the sleepless couple that, while they might be sorry for the inconvenience they were causing, they'd come to the conclusion, through prayerful consideration, that God had chosen them to inspire others to find the true, but sadly lost, meaning of Christmas. They pointed to the growing stream of visitors each night as evidence that this was right. So rather than politely turning off the offending star at a reasonable hour each evening, it stayed on all night, every night the following week. The police were called out, but they had no better success at convincing the owners of the display to cooperate. Lawsuits were threatened, but the insurance executive and his wife knew that it would take weeks or months for the courts to settle the issue, and by then, the lights would have been taken down and the point moot.

The newspaper reporter who'd written the original piece about the decorations was alerted to the feud, and the story quickly became the most talked-about issue in town, starting a citywide debate about religious rights, property rights, and common courtesy. Opinions, based on emotional letters to the editor, showed nearly even support for both neighbors.

Six days before Christmas, in the middle of the night, a loud popping noise awakened residents of several homes along the street where the controversy occurred. Someone, it turned out, had shot and destroyed the ersatz Star of Bethlehem. The insurance executive was immediately accused, but he denied it vehemently and no evidence was ever produced to link him to the shooting.

Despite this, two days later, when going outside to retrieve his morning paper, the executive discovered his Lexus sedan had four slashed tires and two shattered windows. Assuming it was the work of his neighbor, he stormed next door and demanded immediate restitution for the damage. The newcomer swore he'd no knowledge of the vandalism, but implied that whoever had, in fact, committed the act had certainly been sent by God to atone for the sacrilege the insurance executive himself had carried out. A shoving match ensued, but the men's wives were able to separate them.

The irate insurance man strode to the back of his own house, to the small, detached garage, and found a sledgehammer he'd used some time ago while building a fence. He marched back to the neighbor's front yard and proceeded to swing the tool at each of the parts of the nativity scene, demolishing the heavy, plaster figures one after another. The owners of the crèche came running out of their house, as did the insurance executive's wife, and together they tried to stop the frenzied destruction. More struggling ensued, and only moments before the police arrived, the insurance executive managed to shove the other man to the ground. He lifted the sledgehammer and swung it backward in order to bring it down on the figure of the Christ child. Unfortunately, the neighbor's wife was standing right behind him and took the force of the hammer directly on the top of her head. Before the ambulance arrived, she was dead.

The insurance executive was arrested and charged with negligent homicide, but because of the mitigating circumstances and the fact that he lacked a prior criminal record, he was released on bail and sent home to await his trial. Two days later, on Christmas morning, distraught over causing the death of the woman and the shame he'd brought on his family, the insurance executive hung himself in his basement. His widow sold their house within three weeks, for far less than its value, and told none of her friends where she was moving. The executive's neighbor, beside himself with grief over his wife's death, would not leave his house after her funeral and left all of the decorations untouched, including the debris from the shattered figures on his lawn. Several months later, responding to complaints from the neighborhood association, the city had to clean it up and billed him for the service. Subsequent to the publicity of these tragedies, the persons who'd shot the star and vandalized the car came forward to confess their crimes.

The neighborhood has only recently returned to something close to its old ambiance, but now if you drive around that area at Christmastime, you will find a section, several blocks wide, where no one decorates their house for the holiday.

2.

Some eight or nine years ago, a young man, the son of a prominent national politician, was attending the small, prestigious university in our city. One day, after noticing a number of homeless persons while driving around town, he decided he needed to do something to help these unfortunates who he felt had, as he'd later tell his roommate, slipped between the holes in society's safety net. Money, he decided, was too easy and too impersonal, and too often misappropriated by those in charge of distributing it. He wanted to do something tangible.

When, after several weeks, he was unable to think of anything specific, it occurred to him that his problem stemmed from not having an adequate understanding of the circumstances in which these homeless people lived day after day. The solution seemed obvious. With spring break approaching, he backed out of an intended trip to Mexico with a group of friends and, instead, made plans to spend the entire week living on the streets of our city, subsisting only on what he received in donations from strangers, or what he could otherwise find. His roommate tried to talk him out of this noble, but foolish, scheme, sensibly explaining that his friend could ultimately do more for the downtrodden by lobbying his father, whom most expected to make a run for the presidency in the next election, to endorse legislation that would improve the lot of the poor in general.

But the young man was undeterred. The final week of school before the break he stopped shaving and began wearing the same clothes each day. On the final day of classes, immediately following his last exam, he went back to his dorm, wrote a note to his roommate wishing him a good time in Mexico, then left campus.

Eight days later, on the evening before classes were to resume, the young man walked into his room at school, disheveled, dirty, and subdued. His roommate, anxious to hear about his friend's social experiment, pressed the young man for details of his week on the streets. The latter was reluctant to talk about it, explaining only that there was a vast subculture of homeless persons, unknown to the majority of people who pass by them everyday without a thought. He wouldn't go into specifics, but did mention that he had befriended a man whom he knew only as T, and that T had, in some way he wouldn't elaborate on, saved his life.

As the new semester began, the young man was unable to concentrate on his studies and skipped classes frequently, sometimes disappearing for hours on end, only to show up in the middle of the night. It wasn't long before he started to be gone for several days at a time. His grades suffered and he was soon at risk of failing out. The roommate, concerned about his friend, called the young man's parents and explained what had occurred and the personality changes that had taken place.

The following weekend, the politician and his wife came to the campus to see their son and to find out what was happening to him. He wasn't in his dorm room and no one knew where he was. They waited there until shortly after midnight, when at last the young man showed up. A loud argument, which was witnessed by many students in the residence hall, ensued involving the young man, his father, and his roommate. There was some pushing and shoving and the young man threatened to kill his father if he didn't leave him alone. The campus police were called, but before they arrived, the young man walked out of the dormitory, ostensibly to cool off. To this day the young man has not been seen again.

When a few days after the fight at school it became obvious that the young man wasn't coming back, his father, using his considerable wealth and political clout, arranged for the FBI and private investigators to track him down. But even with these extensive resources, no trace of the young man was found. The homeless man known as T was identified and located. He was found wearing a sweatshirt that had belonged to the young man. T was taken into custody and questioned at length, but he was unable to provide any information that could help in determining where the young man had gone.

Months later, blaming himself for his son's disappearance, the young man's father quit politics in order to spend all of his time looking for his son. He used up most of a considerable fortune following any lead, no matter how dubious, driving and flying all over the country over the course of the next five years. The frustration of this fruitless mission began to take its toll, both financially and emotionally. The young man's parents were forced to sell their huge home and move into a small house in a rundown part of the city. They both began to drink heavily, which undoubtedly played a significant role in the automobile accident in which they were killed.

It was thought by many that the funeral of his parents would be the incentive that would bring the young man out of hiding and back to our city. However, it is not known whether or not he even learned of their deaths, because he never showed up. Many assumed that he, too, had died: a victim of the streets.

Each year our local newspaper now runs a story about this mysterious young man and how his disappearance may have inadvertently changed the course of our nation's history—a speculative piece full of whys and what-ifs about how different things might have been had his father stayed in politics and been elected president, an assumption that seemed to gain more certainty after his death than it ever had while he was alive. And this story would have slipped into the status of nothing more than interesting local legend had a caretaker at the cemetery not noticed some of the objects on the grave of the young man's parents. He found two fresh white roses and a small sign made from a piece of cardboard. The sign, printed with black marker, read, "Please Help. Anything Will Do. God Bless." A handwriting expert studied the sign and concluded that, based on a comparison to samples from old college notes, it was nearly certain that the sign had indeed been written by the couple's son. The freshness of the roses, too, indicated that the items had been placed that same day.

Nothing else has ever been found on the grave, and it's been two years since the flowers and sign were discovered, but many people here (including myself) find themselves stopping now whenever they see homeless persons. We give them money while studying their faces, each of us certain we'll be the one to discover, at last, the missing college student.

3.
Twelve years ago my wife and I bought a house beyond the northern limits of the city. We loved this house as much as people can love such things, and shared enjoyment and pride in taking care of it over the years. It sits atop a rise on a large, wooded lot in what was, at the time we moved in, a planned development. While not restricted in the way a gated community would be, its exclusivity stemmed from simple economics: average families couldn't afford these properties. And, technically, neither could we. But we were young, childless professionals who harbored unbridled optimism concerning our future and figured that if

we struggled a little for a few years, our success would soon provide the means to transform our home from a financial burden to a sound investment. As it turned out, we were right. In less than five years, both my wife and I were earning six-figure salaries.

The most appealing of the house's attributes was the most basic—location. It was outside the city in a rustic section of the county, yet our development's entrance was situated on a main highway connecting with the nterstate, which provided quick access to anywhere in town. Most days I could leave our house and be in my downtown office in less than fifteen minutes. To this day, despite the insidious advance of the city limits, the house enjoys relative isolation accorded by a buffer of untouched woods that surround the small, private community. And although I witnessed increasing growth along the highway as I made my daily commute to work, the only intersecting road close to the house is a narrow, dirt lane that curves into the woods, remarkable to me only as a valuable landmark that I used when giving directions to our place, since it is exactly eight-tenths of a mile from the entrance to the development.

Like so many things that our eyes stop seeing after they become familiar, this unmarked road soon went unnoticed as I sped past on my way to and from town. There were never, that I have witnessed, any cars going down or coming from it, and I unconsciously assumed it was an old hunting path or shortcut to some place I never even bothered trying to imagine.

One Saturday six months ago, our daughter (who is two weeks from turning seven as I write this) was riding in the back of our minivan. I'd just picked her up from a friend's birthday party and she was unusually quiet. I assumed she'd worn herself out playing and, in fact, she seemed droopy-eyed when I peeked at her in the rearview mirror. So it startled me when, passing the dirt road eight-tenths of a mile from home, she asked if we could stop and walk down it. I started to ask why, but instead made a U-turn at the entrance to our development and parked on the narrow gravel shoulder across from the path.

The early December sky was a brittle blue with big puffy clouds barely moving. The air was crisp without being cold, the kind of air that brings everything into sharp focus. As we walked along the hard, red clay road, I held my daughter's hand. The road curved to the right and then again to the left, disappearing deep into the woods. We hadn't gone more than half a mile when I could no longer hear cars from the highway where our car was parked. I glanced down at my daughter, who looked up and smiled, but I couldn't tell if it was an excited or a nervous smile.

We ventured farther into the woods, the naked maples and oaks standing in harsh contrast to the durable green of the pines. The trees seemed to close around us, and the road's end was nowhere in sight. I mentioned to my daughter that the road was likely a dead end and that we'd probably seen most, if not all, there was to see. And had I stopped right there and turned us around, I know things would be different now. But we kept walking just a bit farther, rounding another bend, and that's when we saw the house.

Actually, my first impression was that it was no more than a shack, perhaps indeed a hunting blind, bolstering my initial suspicion about the purpose of the road. Except that a thin, steady line of smoke rose from a pipe vent that angled up from the tin roof. The walls of the structure were simple boards and I could not see any windows. I stared at the ramshackle building, trying to reconcile my assessment that no one could possibly live in such a place with the sight of the smoke streaming from the chimney. I was about to tell my daughter that we needed to turn back when a man carrying an armload of sticks and branches came around the far side of the house. He was thin and walked bent forward, like the burden of the sticks was great. From where we stood, his eyes were no more than shadows set deep in his face above the sharp ridges of cheekbones that were, to my reckoning, sickeningly prominent.

When he noticed us, the old man stopped briefly, then continued into the house with his load of kindling. I waited to see if he would come back to find out who we were once he'd relieved himself of his load, but he didn't. I looked at my daughter and could see the unspoken questions in her eyes. We turned and walked back to the car. Once buckled in her seat, my daughter asked me if I thought the man actually lived in that house. I said I doubted it, telling my first real lie to her.

I was unable to shake the image of the gaunt stranger (my neighbor, I realized), and for weeks, whenever I passed the dirt road, I would slow down, hoping to catch a glimpse of him. My daughter seemed to forget about the man in the flimsy shack and we never again spoke of him. I didn't mention him to my wife.

In late January our area was hit with an ice storm. For two days I didn't sleep, worried about the man in the woods. Once, in the middle of the night, I even climbed into my SUV and drove to the road and started walking down it, but chickened out, compounding my guilt and anxiety.

I know I should just take a walk down the dirt road and see for myself that the old man is fine. But I keep asking myself, what if he isn't? Who knew he was there—and could have helped him—besides me? Is it worse to know, or not to know? These questions paralyze me. And now my lack of sleep has begun to take its toll; I've became irritable. My wife and I fight often about little things, about nothing. I haven't been able to concentrate at the office and today my boss suggested I use some vacation time to get myself together. I'm thinking of quitting instead.

I don't know what I'll do or where I'll go if that happens, but I do know that, no matter what, I won't complain.

The Dictionary as Field Guide
Christopher Cokinos

Jack Stephens nursed the Toyota HiLux pickup truck along the unpaved mountain road above Thule Air Force Base in Greenland. In this austere, rocky expanse, we had just passed, of all things, a traffic sign—a yellow diamond with the black-lettered word *Slow*—and I asked Jack to stop. I wanted a picture of it, for, in the distance below, amazingly, strangely, lay the brown fell-fields and, farther on, like a permanent cloud, the Greenland ice cap. I got out of the truck. Just where metaphoric cloud and literal cloud met was hard to discern. The world turned white there, and for seconds I could not move. Was there a faint blue line separating earth from sky? I twitched my head, framed the shot, pressed a button. Hundreds of miles north of the Arctic Circle, on a mountain with just two humans, here I was taking a picture of a traffic sign, of a single word—exact and evocative—that, much later, would lead me to muse on some unexpected and strange evolutions of language. Mesmerized, I kept looking at peeled yellow paint and the unfamiliar world thereafter, that caution and panorama. Jack waited patiently.

I hadn't exactly come for this. Working on a book about meteorites, I would travel soon with researchers from the Peregrine Fund, which operates a scientific enclave at this American air base. I'd travel by open boat—it would take three trips because of mechanical problems and a biologist's rock-gashed hand—but we'd find the obscure locations where explorer Robert Peary had retrieved three massive meteorites in the 1890s. While P-fund researchers surveyed for falcons, I'd retrace footsteps in order to explore obsessions with meteorites. But before the *Barb* ("Big Assed Red Boat") was ready, I had time to explore land beyond the metal-and-pipe-laden base. Jack, the Thule meteorologist and P-fund site coordinator, showed me ice cap, icebergs, glacier, bay and ocean from on high, broken foundations, and cables flung along the ground because they could not be buried in the frozen earth. They stretched everywhere, like the filaments of a spider web.

Alone one day, I would watch storms over Dundas, a now-empty village that was once home to commerce—a trading post. Those red-and-green buildings, squat, wooden, and simple, were then the only bright human colors in the landscape. There was orange lichen on rocks and on a single headstone for a long-dead, forgotten sailor. Pre-storm dark seemed both to mute and to vivify the orange.

I had wanted, almost desperately, to write about something that did not touch, let alone ruminate on, ecological relation and ruin. For years, those words seemed to go hand in hand, like desire and shame. As Aldo Leopold wrote, once you know a landscape ecologically, you see not only its beauty but also its wounds. After years of researching extinct birds for my first nonfiction book, I needed to move beyond such losses. My fascination with the night sky had helped me cope (surely we cannot sully every planet), and watching shooting stars led me to write about them and their larger kin. I found the science and stories of meteorites a delight—and an escape.

I pressed another button, the lens retracted, and I clambered into the truck.

My wish had been naïve: The meteorite project kept sending me to actual locales and their literal and metaphorical ecologies. Wind in his white hair, Jack showed me this dry land between ice sheet and arctic waters—those bewildering immensities—and spoke in a soft southern accent about snow buntings, the musk oxen at Cape Atholl (we didn't see them), years of living at Thule, troublesome sediments in the base's drinking water and his solution to *all* environmental problems.

"An asteroid whack would be good for the human race," Jack remarked casually. The pickup rumbled along. His words jostled in the air.

Not a planet-killer, mind you, but a smaller hit, one that would serve as a catalyst to move industrial civilization from the Earth to the moon, Mars, and the asteroid belts. Such a relocation, he reasoned, would allow us to continue to extract resources for increased quality of life while at the same time leaving Earth free of further degradation. If Robert Frost was right—that Earth is the right place for love—then Lacus Autumni may be the right place for smelting.

The industrialization of space not a new idea—it's the ultimate form of "off-shoring"—and I recognize the near-term impracticality of putting mines and factories, not to mention farms, in space. Still, I find the idea oddly compelling. It appeals to my romantic-adventuresome streak, the one that lets me stare at musty color plates of 1950s space artist Chesley Bonestell, his renderings of astronauts tumbling over Deimos with canal-crossed Mars looming above, of pliers and martini glasses floating in a ship bound for the moon. When I was a child I always planned to build a mock-up of a Gemini capsule and pretend to fly. But I was never very good at using tools, and eventually Miss Hawk kicked me out of advanced algebra.

Months after returning from Greenland, in my new home in northern Utah, while daily pulling thistle from beside the Blacksmith Fork River, while nightly watching the Milky Way stream across midnight mountains that rise near the house, I began to understand that the traffic sign on the mountain and Jack's offhand remark not only had prompted a nostalgia for cosmic development but also had forced me to think about first things, first principles, about my own conceptions of why nature matters and how: that is, what we talk about when we talk about nature.

I had only just begun to adjust to living in the Rockies instead of the tallgrass prairie of Kansas, where for a decade and a half I'd rooted myself as a writer, teacher, birder, and activist. Outside my kitchen window, in Nibley, Utah, a curving sweep of benches formed by the varied levels of ancient Lake Bonneville reminded me of the flat-topped Flint Hills of Kansas, though what grows in the Cache Valley is sage and rabbitbrush, sego lily, and Rocky Mountain juniper, not big bluestem, not blue false indigo, not osage orange. James McMurtry's song "I'm Not from Here, I Just Live Here" kept playing on my stereo and in my mind. My partner, Kathe, and I knew we had a lot to learn about our home—knowing the place we're in is important to us—and, though I wished for no asteroid impact, I did want to explore what seemed implicit in Jack's rationale for a space-based economy: that nature is both source and solace. My first summer beside the river—ceiling fans whirring, blinds drawn down against a heat long-time locals said was warmer than usual—I felt that my conversation with Jack also had something to do with my inability to name all the new trees or puzzle out new bird songs, and my exhilaration over the prospect of learning them.

From aquifers to the nitrogen cycle, the nonhuman world is a storehouse of things and processes, and we use them in order to live. From sigh-inducing vistas to the connective rhythms of seasonal change, the nonhuman world is also a psychological comfort to our savannah-evolved selves. Our present use of nature threatens, of course, this two-fold utility, and far beyond merely relaying this familiar news, language can help return our bodies to places and our places to us. It can hone a saving precision. Words remember what we forget. "Body" arises from the German for, of all things, a brewing tub, which itself links back to *apotheca*, the Latin for "storehouse." And the word life relates to the German *leib* or "body." Words have a kind of muscle memory, and the dictionary is a field guide, is a history.

Consider "need." The Indo-European root of "need" includes a base *neu-* that means "to collapse with starvation." Postmodernist and capitalist skepticism about the importance of nonhuman nature, let alone its existence, tends to fall away when you throw a rock at the questioning professor's head (probably your grade drops too). More radically, such doubt is meaningless when your body has no more fat, the well is dry, the village crops have failed, and rebels have plundered rations at the border. If neoterics frequently mistake conveniences for needs (I can; witness my upset at a broken water heater last week), then the body's demands—for air, water, food, relief, sex, pleasure, beauty, health, a good life, and a comfortable end—remind us that these are the baseline necessities.

Intellectual skepticism thrives best, after all, on two thousand calories a day.

The lungs of a Bangalore computer programmer and the lungs of a Liverpool panhandler both have what might be called a stakeholder interest in oxygen. The Vancouver paper-products executive and the Portland tree-spiker—as well as the trees they are interested in—share a requirement for water. From hovel to skyscraper, we feel hunger, satisfy it (or not), urinate, defecate, sleep, fornicate. We need nature because we *are* nature. This is not trivial. We are animals. Human culture has been trying to walk away from that fact for a long time. We've been doing the walking with our syllogisms and our citified feet.

We are blessed and cursed to be thinking animals. And everyone knows—right?—that we're not the only creatures who can learn language, feel grief, or use tools. We are, however, the only creatures whose tools can lead us to express grief. Although we evolved to sense and to respond to our immediate surroundings—where consequences can be fire-fast—we now have expanded our perception to include our less-immediate surroundings, from the microscopic to the macroscopic, from three dozen species of *Prochlorococcus* to fossil energy from the Big Bang. We swap out genes, run cars on hydrogen, and propose to unfurl cooling sails above the Earth. Some of us want to wear computer screens just above our eyes, in order to walk while reading email scrimming over the world. Like a Bach toccata and fugue, though not as beautiful, this is impressive, if intimidating, stuff.

On good days, I think that careful conversation and conservation will allow us to remember that the ability to do something is not in itself a justification for doing it. I think that we can alter economic practices to recognize, as sustainability visionary and businessman Paul Hawken does, the Earth's existence as a closed system (with the exception of sunlight). I think that we can raise living standards for the rest of the world while drastically reducing associated ecological waste. Hawken calls for a "restorative economics," one in which businesses and governments become "more environmentally accurate and culturally enduring." ("Accurate," "care," "cure," "curiosity"—all are etymologically related.) Hawken cites as one part of this transformation 3M's "Pollution Prevention Pays" mandate, which has saved the company about half a billion dollars while significantly cutting solid-waste, air, and water pollution. I think of a recent business publication that featured a balanced and foreboding cover story on the dangers of global climate change. At the time I write this, in the early years of the twenty-first century, even wary politicians of America's most conservative bent are beginning to take notice.

On bad days—when, say, I read of Australia's biodiversity bloodletting before I have gone to my writing desk—I think such re-education and retooling won't keep pace with mass extinction. We are living into being the sixth great mass extinction in the history of the planet. *We* are the killer asteroid. We may end with ravaged biomes over whose scraps we fight, night-vision drones versus car bombs. Bureaucrats and terrorists may set aside their concerns over fourth-quarter earnings and heaven, respectively, and instead duke it out over access to aquifers (drinking water) and rainforests (pharmaceutical warehouses). Sometimes I take dark comfort in geologic time, that vast stretch of epochs free of bungling bipeds, those eons during which most species disappear only to be replaced by new ones. As the bumper sticker says, "Nature Bats Last." Meanwhile, I thrill at the discovery of new planets around long-charted suns, remaining hopeful that telescopes soon will pluck a bushel and a peck of Earth-like worlds throughout the galaxy.

Such a mingling of nihilism and yearning solves nothing grand, but it can help me with the daily news and return me to the day at hand, which now is sunlight and a breeze aloft, helping to break a winter inversion during which the valley's air has filled with soot, car exhaust, and cow farts. For a time this winter, the Cache Valley had worse air than major cities throughout the United States. The day is also a birdsong I have come to know and need: that of the river-loving American Dipper, who sings even in bleak midwinter.

A prominent American nature writer once told me that he'd just returned from New York City where, meeting with businessmen in an apartment—I imagine a spacious, minimally decorated loft with two walls of floor-to-ceiling windows—they "talked about how to save the world. Really." I believe him. I hope they have it figured out. Over the years since that conversation, the book I wrote on vanished North American birds led some people to write me heartfelt, encouraging letters; mostly these came from birders and activists but one, handwritten, came from the governor of New York. Those letters also renew my sense of commitment and optimism. I recall, though, in my role as activist for my local Audubon chapter in northeastern Kansas, years ago, I once deeply offended a farmer. Condescending to him, I had said that I was glad that "folks like him" were also interested in finding ways to save the tiny, endangered Topeka Shiner. Another time, in an auditorium packed with citizens upset by plans to build a road through tallgrass that was home to prairie chickens, dickcissels, and milkweed, a county commissioner asked me if I were a hypocrite for living in a house and wanting other people "to live in teepees." I had nothing constructive to say in either instance.

I no longer believe that self-righteousness is a synonym for resolve. Not long ago, Kathe and I joined some biologists, a rancher, and a couple of his employees and drove four-wheelers over his family's vast ranch in the high Bear River Range at the southern end of the valley. We were looking for boreal toads, a creature, which, if found, might eventually limit what the rancher could do with his property—something he didn't mind because it also would make it well-nigh-impossible for developers to run a road across his land to a ski resort.

What is progress to some is mucking up to others and vice versa. Environmentalists rightly question the consequences of technological advances, but often wrongly assume that any advance will prove itself deleterious to the rest of creation, if not us. Technocrats rightly search for ways to improve quality of life, but often wrongly believe that all such improvements are necessary and should immediately benefit only humans, especially those in American suburbs. We didn't find any boreal toads, but Kathe came just a few toes away from the biggest bull snake most of us had ever seen, and I savored hearing and seeing a yellow-breasted chat at lunch. Kathe and I felt that day those glimmers of connective sustenance—community—that meant we were making a home.

How can we answer questions about what passes for progress if we forget ancient roots? It's worth recalling that from the Greek *oikos*—house—emerge the words economy and ecology. "Human," "humus," "homage"—all grow up from the Indo-European word *ghom-:* Earth. Ground.

Where does your water come from? Where did your dinner come from? Where does your trash go? What powers your furnace? How do you like to be touched? Such questions can remind us of our deepest necessities and how they are—or can be—met. They remind us of consequence and of responsibility. An environmentally accurate relationship begins with the home of the body and the body at home. Only then can we speak with precision.

Learning such accuracy need not be a grim self-education, one laden with First-World guilt. A three-year-old named Ben recently stood in my yard entranced by blizzards of cabbage butterflies flitting about in a lavender bush (both species are, I've learned, naturalized). Delight is a teacher.

I once bewildered and amused my students when I pointed to a classroom's carpet and said, "That's an ecosystem too." We all agreed later that the campus, with its exotic and water-hungry plants, as well as the native juniper and Douglas fir forests of the nearby mountains, are more satisfying than blue carpet. That preference, like Ben's, bears testament to our need for affinitive relationships with non-built environments. Sociobiologist E. O. Wilson calls it "biophilia." It helps explain why office workers want plants in their cubicles. It helps explain pets, postcard views, and communities that agitate for open space. A well-fed body still craves a green and beautiful world. The body is home, is world, is of home, of world. Deep in the word "world" are German compounds for man and for age.

Perhaps a lovely red bird calls in your backyard but you do not know its name. Still it calms you. Perhaps its presence fills some lack, gives flashes of wonder in the leaves. Perhaps it is a scarlet tanager, which winters in rainforests bordering a coffee plantation that provided the beans you brewed with breakfast while listening to the bird. Right here we are led afar and back again. An environmentally accurate relationship must start with where you live and how you speak of it, because without an accurate relationship to the local, one can live as though places, like trash, were disposable. Environmental accuracy means taking the time to learn particulars, to learn proper nouns.

Wel-, an Indo-European base, means "to roll or turn" and relates to "valley" and "walk" and "well" and "willow."

Euphemism, passive voice, abstraction—these tend to be tools of the powerfully distant (as well as the locally ignorant), tools that efface the particular the way an unwanted and unannounced backhoe trespasses to scrape a riverbank clear of "brush" (wood's rose, box elder, peach leaf willow). We know the dangers of euphemism, passive voice, and abstraction especially during times of war. Officials speak of "collateral damage" when they mean innocent dead. They say "Mistakes were made" to avoid responsibility. They speak of "threats to freedom" to justify undermining our own liberty. But consider a term apparently innocuous, such as "housing starts." Seen in a national context, that term is merely the title of some statistic, some "gauge of economic activity." But for an actual hillside in, say, Saint George, Utah, a "housing start" is the extinction of a colony of the endemic bear claw poppy or, perhaps, a neocolonial set upon unstable blue clay by an unwary developer.

George Orwell, in his essay "Politics and the English Language," equated *thinking* with *seeing*, remarking that our language "becomes ugly and inaccurate because our thoughts are foolish." This is a feedback loop, to adopt a term he might not have approved of. "The slovenliness of our language makes it easier for us to have foolish thoughts," he continued. Eyes that can't see the particulars of a place degrade both thought and diction, leading near and far to "vagueness and sheer incompetence" in speech and in action.

In Greenland, while visiting a remote Inuit village called Savissivik,

I learned that environmentalists, like loan officers, can fall prey to wielding language over great distances to harmful effect. Greenpeace campaigns against whaling and sealing years ago had failed to take into account the subsistence needs of the Inuit. A hunting people still intimately bound with what the land and seas provide, the Inuit remain legitimately angry at well-heeled activists more familiar with which aisle has the organic basalmic vinegar than, say, flensing a seal in order to feed a family during an Arctic winter.

The Inuit also remind us that television can wreak devastating effects on people and communities; alcoholism, domestic abuse, and malaise have increased where television has appeared in native communities previously unconnected from Hollywood and its imitators. Global culture's fast-moving images divert us from slow-paced questioning, walking, and naming—the basis of the education of the body and the body's place, the basis of environmental accuracy—while reinforcing particularity mostly in reference to products and celebrities. I shop and watch TV too, but I try not to mistake that realm for the one that undergirds it.

Not from television did we learn that the yellow sheen Kathe and I admired on the mountainsides when we arrived from Kansas is, in fact, the water-sucking Dyer's woad, an exotic with no value for the land. Not from catalogs did we learn that Russian olive trees are also lovely and not to be planted. From our billing statements, we've learned that water is crazy-cheap in this, the second-driest state in the country. We're in the sixth year of a drought, nearly a once-in-five-hundred-years event, or so the experts say.

The body, language, and place can root and connect us in ways that proffer humility, even grace, traits that make the resolution of our difficulties—climate change, mass extinction, hunger—if not perfect for both human and nonhuman realms, then at least honorable, for having been suffused with care and nuance. This approach can ramify our dilemmas—save this or destroy that?—into something more complex, something truer to reality. If we take the time to know ourselves in places, if we take the time to learn the language of such knowledge, then we will be forced by the interconnectedness of living things to speak with greater care, and that will take us out of the false choices of dilemmas and into the realm of predicament. If we are to make it around the curve, we may need to take some things slowly.

Slowness often feels counterintuitive, however, because there are problems we can solve quickly, if we redirect energy, attention, and money. Imagine what the Pentagon's seven billion dollars spent on a helicopter project might have done for wetlands restoration, promotion of sustainable urban design, or photovoltaic efficiency research. If someone were to come up with a practicable and ecologically sound plan to quickly halt global warming—those sails in space! carbon sequestering!—I wouldn't oppose it.

I worry, though, at our capacity to fetishize speed, not only because unintended consequences often follow quickly on the heels of quick solutions, but also because fast-paced "problem solving" is part and parcel with fast-track syntax—that is, with oversimplification. Do we need nuclear power or not? Do we need genetically modified crops or not? Do we need cars or not? Do we need wind-power farms or not? Do we need prairie dogs or not? Talk-show syntax never leads to solutions.

Conservatives (though Teddy Roosevelt wouldn't have called them that) frequently employ similar kinds of questions: "Which is more important—loggers or spotted owls?" "Which is more important—eliminating disease-carrying mosquitos or protecting the eggshells of birds?" "Which matters more, us or some damn fish?" That is: Which do we value more, humans or nature?

The core supposition—that we are separate from nature—ought to raise eyebrows. Yet even the most sophisticated liberals can engage in such thinking. The French philosopher Bernard-Henri Levy, a social activist, celebrity, and son of a lumber executive, recently told *Vanity Fair*, "I loathe what is natural. I think the more laws a society has, the more livable it is . . . . It is a form of idolatry to sanctify stone, earth. Men are holy, not stones." He might as well have said "not honeybees" or "not yew trees." But this is not the place for a discourse on pollination or cancer.

It's another Greenland image that tells me that all these either/or linguistic constructions are dangerous because they are inaccurate and thus deepen the gulf between humans and the places, processes, creatures, and sentences that sustain us. When I look at pictures of the small boat that carried me through the icy waters of Melville Bay, along the Cape York coast, I think of stories of survival in such craft, survival in small boats surrounded by big water. I take the pictures down from a file and look at them by my window view of the Bear River Range: my new home. The southern slopes have already lost their snow, at least at the lower elevations. Everywhere, snowpack is less than normal. Though I don't know it yet, March will come on hot and fast, melting snow so quickly that streams and rivers won't recharge their flows as they typically do. The word kin has as its Indo-European base *gen-, "to produce," from which stream relations to "genus" and "genesis." A version of this base, meaning "to give birth to; produce," leads to our much-used and little-thought-of word, nature. Somewhere along the Blacksmith Fork a kingfisher keeps watch below. Somewhere in the valley a farmer is signing papers that will give him a retirement and his former pasture a crop of condos. Deep in the word separate are *se-*, "apart," and *parare*, "to set in order," related to *parere*, "to bring forth"; so separation is the end of bringing forth. Separation is extinction.

For the first time in days, the sun is shining, and I think now that asking whether people matter more than nature is like asking survivors in a lifeboat what matters most: their lives or the lifeboat?

Vaguely Listening to Something in Italian Played through an Intercom
Tony Hoagland

One more Saturday night and you're by yourself again,
standing in a restaurant on College Avenue
holding a slice of pizza in your hand,
and reading the giant menu on the flyspecked wall,

when halfway through the song, the words start
creeping into your head
because if you are not mistaken it seems the singer
is addressing Solitude

and not only that & he's thanking her
for holding him so close last night,
for touching him in places that only she could reach—

You decide that loneliness must be a more developed art form in Italy
than in southeastern Texas,
and from the little you know of opera, that seems quite possible

what with all those fat men getting up on stage
to yodel out their mamma mias,
their antipastos, and solo mios.
You have never been to Italy, but you

can comprendo that redollent mixture
of beauty and suffering.
You too have ridden the ferris wheel alone,

and hung on tight in that difficult moment
of watching the waiter remove
the second set of silverware.

Tony Hoagland

And now you remember the slice of pizza in your hand,
and notice the shape your teeth have cut out of it,
how anonymous that bitemark is,

how poignant and forlorn.
Already you can tell how empty you are going to feel
when the song is really over

and you are back in this ordinary pizza parlour
with the plastic Parmesan dispensers
and its vulgar North American flies.

You thought for a moment you had understood
something about suffering,
how it exists for a reason;

but the insight was just like your life,
which slips out of your grasp
each time you think you have a grip on it,

which hovers like a mist in front of you,
then drifts away—
always a little beyond your comprehension,

always a little hidden—
which, as any real Italian could tell you,
will always be the case

with something in translation.

Noon
TONY HOAGLAND

Noon at the gym,
and work-ethic Nichole is giving a class called *Tight Butt*
for women who fear their husbands
are losing interest,
and others who are part of
the Husband Recycling Program.

Fifty serious minutes of sweat,
repetitive step and thigh burn,
a techno & trance drill sergeant—
There will always be some who motivate by flattery,
but Nichole is a punisher.

I am watching the guy on the rowing machine
who is stroking across a cardiovascular ocean
while watching the backside of a redheaded woman
who is using her lunch break to catch up
on furniture catalogues.

Did he who made the lamb
make the three or four of us? and what was he thinking,
when he fastened our pieces together?
snapped on the plastic back and set us in motion?

I myself am not a pretty sight,
with my red face and little belly
running through a mirror toward my grave

but perhaps I am an advertisement
for not trying to improve;

or an advertisement for trying in spite of certain failure,
or an advertisement for joining the conspiracy

that seems to exist between us
to never, ever stop craving.

Three Maps
CLYDE EDGERTON

From three novels: *Red Eye* (terrain), *Where Trouble Sleeps* (town), and *Lunch at the Piccadilly* (narrative in progress)

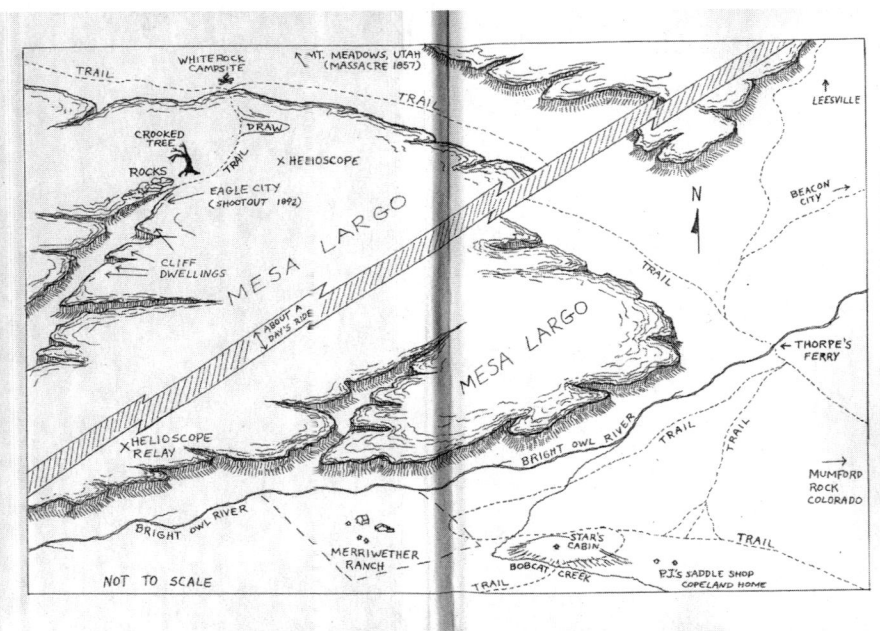

Clyde Edgerton

The Blinker Light in Listre – 1950

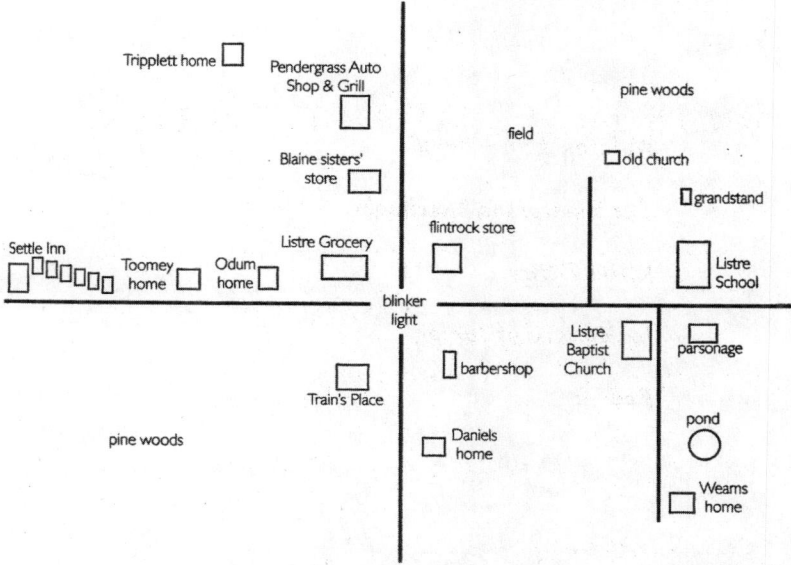

The Stoplights at Hunter's Grove – 2000

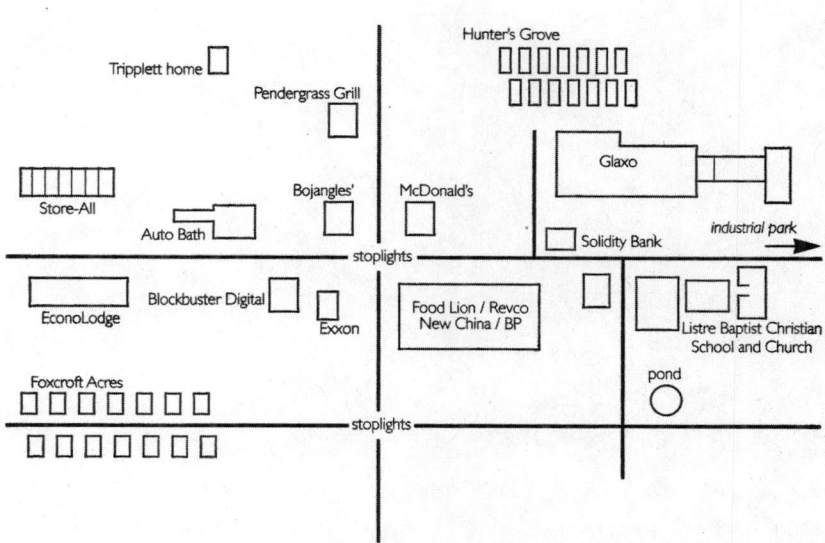

Ecotone: reimagining place

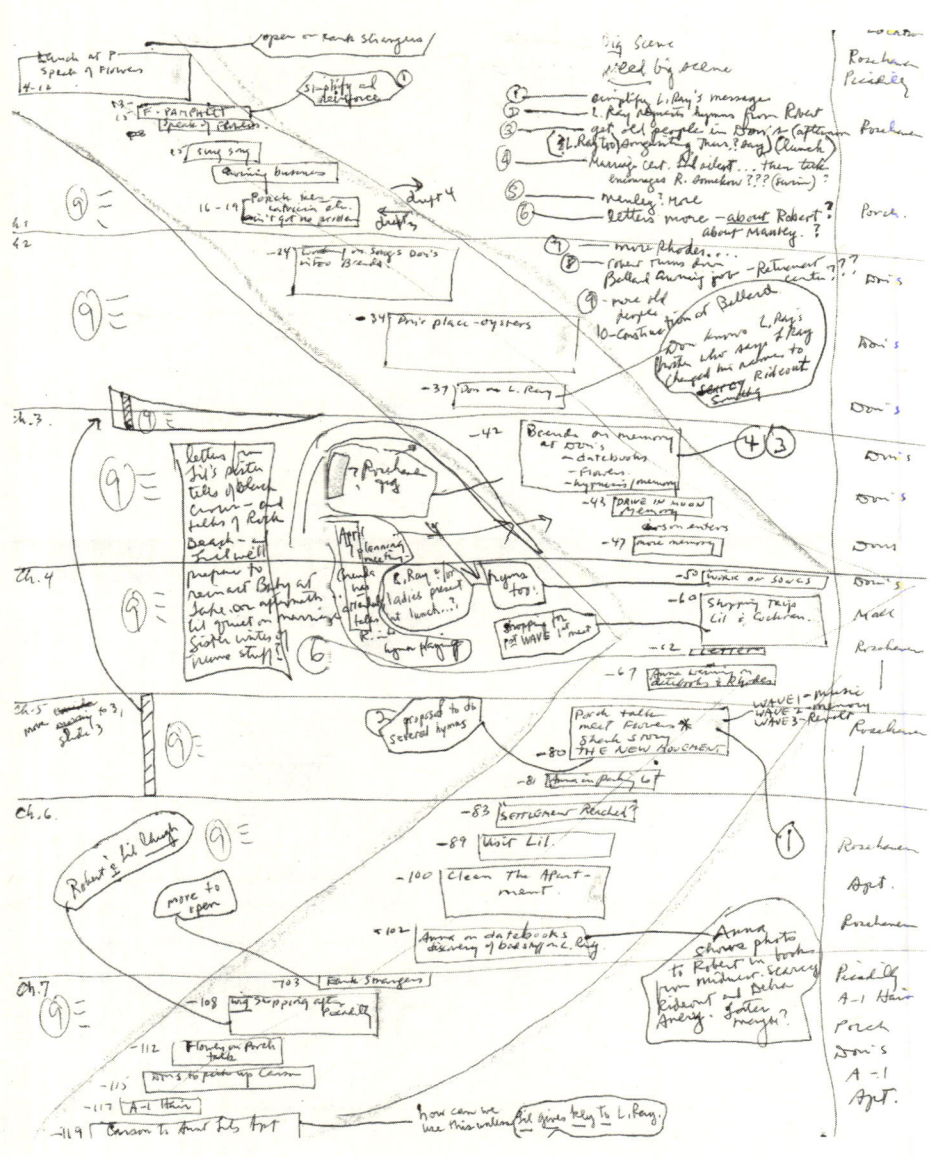

Clyde Edgerton

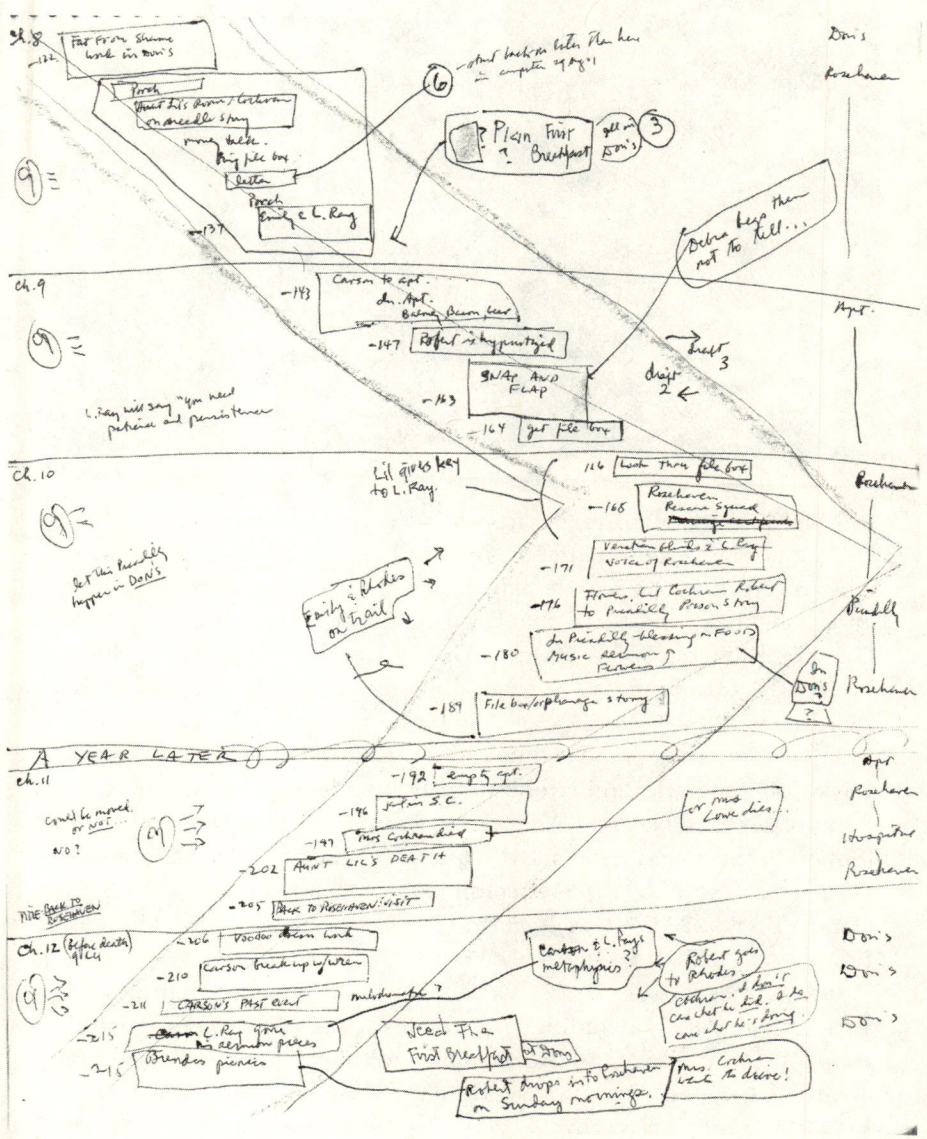

The Ecotone interview

Bill McKibben is a writer, environmentalist, and founder of Step It Up 2007, an organization that sponsored rallies in hundreds of American cities on April 14, 2007, to demand that Congress enact curbs on carbon emissions that would cut global warming pollution eighty percent by 2050. McKibben's books include *The End of Nature* (Random House, 1989); *The Comforting Whirlwind: God, Job, and the Scale of Creation* (Eerdmans, 1994); *The Age of Missing Information* (Random House, 1995), a comparison between twenty-four hours of one hundred cable television programs and twenty-four hours on an Adirondack mountaintop; *Hope, Human and Wild* (Little, Brown, & Co., 1995); *Maybe One* (Simon & Schuster, 1998), a discourse on human population; *Long Distance: A Year of Living Strenuously* (Simon & Schuster, 2000); *Enough* (Times Books, 2003); and *Wandering Home* (Crown, 2005). His most recent book is *Deep Economy: the Wealth of Communities and the Durable Future* (Times Books, 2007). McKibben is a frequent contributor to various magazines, including *The New York Times*, *The Atlantic Monthly*, *Harper's*, *Orion*, *The New Yorker*, *Granta*, and *Rolling Stone*. He has been awarded Guggenheim and Lyndhurst Fellowships and the Lannan Prize for nonfiction writing. In 2006, McKibben helped lead a five-day walk across Vermont to demand action on global warming. He currently resides in Ripton, Vermont.

with Bill McKibben
DAVID GESSNER

David Gessner: Believe it or not, we are only a couple years away from the twentieth anniversary of the publication of *The End of Nature*. In that book, your first, you presented a powerful overview of the science of global warming, and an implicit (and explicit) argument that something had to be done about it immediately. Well, here we are two decades after you were researching that book and not a lot has been done. Just a couple of days ago an international scientific study called global warming "irrefutable," but the majority of Americans still don't believe such a thing as global warming exists. Al Gore has a hit movie but policy, if anything, seems to have gone backward.

What do you make of where we are right now? I have read enough of your work to know that you are no Cassandra, but has there been a personal frustration in having this knowledge and seeing others ignore it? Hope has been a theme of your work but there must be periods where you feel some hopelessness at people's unwillingness to see the evidence in front of them.

Bill McKibben: For long periods I have, I confess, despaired a little. I never thought it would be easy (*The End of Nature* is not exactly an upbeat title) but I've been dismayed by how little has happened, how easily the powers that be have swept the problem under the rug. But those days are over. We're clearly making real progress in the last couple of years—hurricane Katrina blew the door open, Al Gore walked through with his movie, and by the time they were done the education process was very nearly complete. Now we're at the movement-building moment, and that's going well too. I kicked off the organizing for a march across Vermont last summer—by its end we had one thousand people walking. Which was a lot for Vermont, but it was also the largest demonstration about global warming yet in this country, and that was pathetic.

With that in mind we launched Stepitup07.org in early January. We asked people to organize rallies in their communities for April 14 (instead of a big march on Washington—too much carbon!). We thought, maybe, we could organize a couple of hundred of these actions. But by mid-February we'd blown by the 650 mark. There are sororities and retirement communities and national environmental groups and churches and rock-climbers and you name it—people were simply waiting for the opening to make their voices heard. It's been unbelievably moving and inspiring.

Gessner: Place has obviously been paramount to you in your life and work. You now teach at Middlebury College, not too far from the Adirondack Mountains that you have written so often about, but not in them. Can you describe how that move came about and what it has meant to you? Has it affected your writing?

McKibben: Well, I've come to think of myself as living in the mountains on either side of Lake Champlain—to imagine it as one large eco-region. That was one of the themes of *Wandering Home,* a book I wrote a couple of years ago about walking from Vermont back to my old house in the Adirondacks. The two sides complement each other nicely—the pastoral and settled and quite beautifully inhabited landscape of Vermont, the wild and beautifully left alone landscape of the Adirondacks. Wendell Berry and Ed Abbey. We need 'em both.

Gessner: This journal concerns itself not just with physical ecotones but also with edges between literary genres. *The End of Nature* established you as one of our best journalistic writers and you have continued to work as a journalist. But elements of the personal essay, the nature essays, and even more personal and spiritual reflections have always made their way into your work, sometimes prominently. Have you enjoyed working these edges between the personal and the objective?

McKibben: I don't think too much about writing, I fear. I have a fairly utilitarian approach—I use what's needed for the task at hand. Sometimes that's facts to appeal to the head, sometimes stories to appeal to other parts of my readers. I've always leaned heavily on reporting—I think telling the tales of others is my greatest pleasure. Finding embers and blowing on them in the hopes sparks will spread.

Gessner: If even the more modest predictions for global warming are correct, then the world now has its back to the wall. In these times is someone who writes about the natural world compelled to be an activist? Ed Abbey, never shy, said that to have convictions and not act on them is moral cowardice. But for many of us, it doesn't seem that simple. Writers tend to be most concerned with the making of sentences, and there are plenty of writers who feel that politics "taints" the work. Some fear being considered "preachy." Is this simply dependent on the temperament of individuals? Or are we at a time when there needs to be a larger compulsion to act? Do writers need to re-awaken to politics beyond the merely literary politics of their own reputations?

McKibben: I don't feel like talking for all writers. For me, activism has been essential from the beginning. And I notice for most of my close friends in the nature writing world that's how it's worked: Terry Tempest Williams in the Utah deserts, Rick Bass defending the Yaak, Richard Nelson in the rainforests of Alaska, Barry Lopez on a hundred fronts, Wendell Berry in the world of agriculture and in defense of the mountains of Kentucky. It's a less ego-filled literary community than some others, I think, because one, we're all outdoors a lot, where it's hard to take yourself that seriously, and two, we know that there are fights that really matter out there.

Gessner: Anyone who writes about trees or bugs tends to get lumped into the environmental writing category, but as you know there are a wide range of writers—Chaucer, say, or Melville—who write about the natural world. But it's safe to say that most of your work—even *Maybe One*—has had at the very least an environmental slant. How did the environment evolve as your subject? Was it always that way? Did you find it or it you? What have been the pleasures and frustrations of being associated with the genre?

McKibben: I read Wendell Berry and I read Ed Abbey and they shook up my mental picture in my mid-twenties (when I was still writing the Talk of the Town for the New Yorker). And I moved to the Adirondacks, and fell in love with big wilderness. And I was journalist enough to recognize that global warming was a big damn story. Most things I've written since have, in some often very tangential way, stemmed from the underlying premise of that book: that we were going to have to change pretty much everything in order to deal with it.

Gessner: I remember once attending a reading with you where Terry Tempest Williams and Barry Lopez, among others, were speaking. Right down the street Wendell Berry was giving a reading. You commented: "If someone dropped a bomb they could wipe out a good percentage of America's nature writers." (That wasn't really a lead in to a question—I just thought it was a funny line.) Anyway, with the Lopezes and Berrys properly enshrined, where does so-called nature writing go next? As a critic of environmental writing, as well as an environmental writer, I would think you would have as good an overview as anyone. One of the goals of this journal has been to reintegrate the genre with just plain writing? Do you see this happening already or in the future? Who are the younger writers in the genre that you find most interesting? What are the less hopeful and the more exciting developments?

McKibben: For the last few months I've been editing, in time I don't really have, the Library of America anthology of American environmental writing. It's been interesting to see the rhythms of it. The most important, Thoreau, was at the very start, and then there were sporadic pulses for a century: Muir and Burroughs, Leopold, Carson. After that things caught fire, and there's been incredible writing ever since. But there's plenty left to be done—the next metaphor is out there, waiting to be captured.

I'm launching a fellowship program in environmental journalism at Middlebury next fall, for early career journalists. They get a couple of weeks of training, and then they go back home with ten grand in research money for the year. We're interpreting journalism pretty broadly—something to do with reporting—and also environmentalism. I think questions about economics, human culture and satisfaction, wealth and poverty, are all central. (They're pretty much the subjects of my new book, *Deep Economy*.)

Gessner: Back to politics. We went to college together during the early Reagan years. Our generation was seen as politically apolitical compared to the one before. But my experience as a college professor tells me that we look like the Chicago Seven compared to students of today.

Have you noted a similar apathy? Do you think it is destined to keep going in this direction or is it more cyclical? Will our current '50s have a '60s?

McKibben: I'm lucky. Middlebury is the most environmentally active college in the country. There are hundreds of kids with a passion for working on these issues, especially climate change, and they are ungodly hardworking and talented. And they seem to be finding allies around the country—there's an awful lot of campus climate organizing going on.

At stepitup07.org we just got a photo from the Alpha Phi sorority chapter at the University of Texas Austin. 180 winsome girls smiling behind their "Cut Carbon 80% by 2050" banner. "We wanted to show it wasn't just hippies who cared," they wrote. Indeed!

Gessner: If we manage to stay on schedule, this journal could be coming out the same week as Step it Up. Could you tell us about the hopes and goals of this effort?

McKibben: To start a people's movement about climate change. And to shift the debate on Capitol Hill in a more ambitious direction. And we're succeeding.

Eight drawings
Anthony Goicolea

The sense of foreboding tinged with playful fantasy, characteristic of many of my photographs, is mimicked in a suite of complex, layered compositions in ink, graphite, paint, and other materials sandwiched between sheets of mylar and plexiglass. Mimicking the layering processes I have used in my previous photographs and digital video editing, I am able to play with opacity, depth of field and scale through the use of collage, tracing and rendering. Drawing and painting gives me an immediate sense of invention and enables a suspension of disbelief.

In my drawings, Figures of indeterminate age and gender pass over and through each other in layered two-dimensional planes of mylar separated by varying thicknesses of plexi-glass. The ghostlike figures are caught in free-floating, awkward, transitional states: sometimes their images are doubled; sometimes they seem as much animal as human. Their bodies fade in and out of each other in a series of tentative lines resembling a palimpsest and referring to memory and transitive states.

These absurd predicaments strive to provoke conflicting emotions in the viewer. Scenes that would normally appear threatening or grotesque, inspire empathy as well as fear, and ultimately are revealed to be more complex than was first assumed.

Disassembly

Balseros

Constellation

Cat's Cradle

Petroleum Dream

Red Sky

Bloodstone

Socioeconomic
Maya Jewell Zeller

Silt muscles out the fish, gold tongues of mica
burn between gills. It's because
of flooding. It's because the schools
needed money for books so the county
let logging roar into the hills. Because
men need jobs. Our family used to eat salmon
every Thanksgiving, our plates alive with sky—
pink orange, peppered meat coating our throats.
One year, when homeless Joe
stayed for dinner, he couldn't stop exclaiming
My god this Chinook is good, so good! My father
had known him for years, and Joe had nowhere
else to go. As he ate his eyes
were billowed and brown, jaw open
to what might float in. Freckles.
But mostly I recall the hands, big-wind hands,
story-telling hands, their waving like fins
treading water.

Eleven Ways to Consider Air
Brandon R. Schrand

I.

Of all the elements in the American West romanticized in the nineteenth century, air is perhaps the most curious. Gold, copper, silver, and water certainly top the list in many ways and rightfully so. The notion of water in the arid West, for instance, lived long (indeed too long) in the Victorian imagination before it was recognized, finally, by some, as a resource with a rarity on par with some hard-rock minerals.

One of the greatest stories about illusory water beyond the one hundredth meridian concerns the Buena Ventura River that supposedly coursed across the alkali desert of western Utah before eventually crashing into the Pacific. Cartographers plotted the river carefully, Mormons told tales of its azure waters, and settlers wandered the desert in vain seeking the faintest sign of its meandering breadth. Trouble is, no such river ever existed despite the stories, despite the maps. It was a myth.

Air, though, was the most egalitarian of elements, and it was purer in the West, people thought, than anywhere else. And it was for the taking. One did not need a sluice box, smelter, or pickax to extract it from the sky. One need not go mad in the desert with a bogus map looking for it. All one needed was a set of lungs to process its infinity.

Seldom did a nineteenth-century travel writer pass through the West without gushing about the pure mountain air. Consider Horace Greeley, who had this to say in his 1860 account, *An Overland Journey*: "Brooks of the purest water murmur and sing in every ravine; springs abound; the air is singularly pure and bracing." Likewise, in *Mountaineering in the Sierra Nevada*, published twelve years later, the swaggering adventure-crat, Clarence King, waxed this way: "After such fatiguing exercises the mind has an almost abnormal clearness: whether this is wholly from within, or due to the intensely vitalizing mountain air, I am not sure." My favorite, albeit lesser known period author, Captain John Codman, traveled west in 1873 and took up lodging in my hometown of Soda Springs, Idaho, a settlement tucked in a sagebrush valley in the southeastern corner of the state. In *The Mormon Country,* published a year later, Codman wrote that in Soda Springs he had "nature in her wild majesty, [and] an elastic, stimulating air."

The mountain air in the West was not there merely to enjoy for its "bracing" freshness; it was literally prescribed for one's health, as if it could be bottled and sold. Silas Weir Mitchell, a physician of prominence toward the end of the nineteenth century, was well known for his "rest cure" (treating women for their so-called "hysteria") and most notably here, for his "fresh air therapy." If a man felt glum, soft, or, god forbid, effete, Mitchell sent him packing for the West where a stark encounter with rugged landscape and exposure to the wild air would restore his machismo faster than he could say "Buena Ventura." Mitchell's most well-known client was none other than Teddy Roosevelt.[1]

It is not known whether John Codman consulted Dr. Mitchell before boarding his Pullman Palace Car to the land of enchanted air, but it is clear that the idea of fresh-air-as-medicine was a priority for the fifty-nine year old blue-blood. His close friend and former Mormon prophet Heber J. Grant once remarked that Codman "suffered from asthma, and he discovered he was better at Soda Springs, Idaho, than at any other place" in the world. The message seemed clear: Go West, old man. Get some air.

II.

During the early summer weeks of 1950, the Monsanto Chemical Company broke ground at the very northern edge of Soda Springs. There, at the northern city limit in a brushy stretch of grazing land amid knuckles and ridges of basalt, the company erected a phosphorus furnace plant above the subterranean layers of ore they planned to reach, exhume, and process. Since that summer, Monsanto has dominated the landscape, economy, and cultural fabric of the southeastern Idaho town. Monsanto *made* the town, people say.

---

[1] If Mitchell were alive today, he might be pleased to know that canned oxygen is now sold over-the-counter and is gaining wide popularity in chic venues known as oxygen bars. Recently, the convenience store Seven-Eleven Japan stocked its shelves with canned oxygen and is now awaiting profits from those seeking a hit of vigor.

Ecotone: reimagining place

And should anyone forget the company's imprint on Soda Springs, custom-made trucks carry cauldrons each filled with six hundred cubic feet of molten, radioactive byproduct, or slag, and slop the refuse down a tailings slope into a waste lagoon.[2] This quasi-lava flow occurs five times an hour, around the clock, day after day, year after year. As a boy growing up there, I used to think it was spectacular, a manmade volcano in my back yard. Actually, the slag's peak temperature is about equal to a volcanic lava flow, topping off at 2,552 degrees Fahrenheit.[3] The slag pours and pours. And the air and the junipers and the silvery sagebrush and the streams and the yawning fields of winter wheat turn wild shades of orange. The townspeople pace the streets and sidewalks daily hunkering under that glow-dome, that pulsing spell of false luminosity. Night becomes day. The daylight is widened. And the air is not elastic or stimulating. It is acrid.

III.
When I was seven, I stopped breathing and was rushed to the emergency room where I was revived on a cold table. I was not in Soda Springs, Idaho, at the time, but in Richland, Washington. We had moved to that desert town two years earlier when my stepdad got a job at the Hanford Nuclear Reactor Project as an electrician. I remember the respirators he brought home and how they made him look terrifying, like an insect.

---

[2] Rock that contains trace elements of elemental phosphorus is processed in the electrical arc-furnaces as a means to extract the phosphorus, while silica and carbon are added to the mix to jettison any impurities. The by-product of this process is a gray, rocky, vitrified slag material that contains uranium and radium. For years, the city of Soda Springs eagerly used the slag as roadfill, foundation mix for schools and houses, sidewalks and bridges. In 1990, the EPA warned residents of Soda Springs that they were at a greater risk of cancer due to the low but ubiquitous levels of radiation around town.

[3] Only once has a man tipped his truck over into the magmatic sludge. I was in high school at the time and remember the day the story spread through town. The unimaginable had happened. That night I drove out to Monsanto and stood in its radiated glow, watching. I was haunted and unendingly fascinated. I imagined how his flesh must have poured from his bones, how the bones became smoke, how the smoke rose in a solitary plume and thinned on an ordinary wind. The slag had erased him. Only the carcass of his truck was recovered. The tragedy did not, however, interrupt the five-count rhythm of the day.

I had cousins who lived in Richland and it was at their house during a sleepover that my respiratory system shut down in the middle of the night. I shot up in bed, straight as a broomstick, and tried to draw a breath, but to no avail. I tried to scream for help but no sound escaped. So I did the next best thing: I pounded on the headboard and walls. I beat my fists into the mattress. In seconds, my aunt Marcia rushed in, while my uncle Jack a police officer, called the ambulance. After that I remember only fragments: the crowded ambulance, its strange half-light, my aunt's gown, hushes, and a hand to my forehead. I wore an oxygen mask the color of seawater. This time I looked like the insect and it was no less terrifying.

In the hospital, I could breathe again. I sat on the cold empty table, feet dangling over the edge, shirtless, my small chest heaving. A doctor orbited the table with a clipboard and stethoscope and asked a battery of questions, most of which my aunt could not answer. My parents, she had said, were on their way. That was the first time I had ever heard the words *asthma attack. Severe.*

Shortly after the attack, Mom scheduled a doctor's appointment where she faced her own barrage of questioning: "Do you or your husband smoke cigarettes?"

"Yes."

"Both of you or just one of you?"

"Both of us."

"Do you smoke in the home or outside?"

"At home. In the home."

Mom, I could tell, was uncomfortable.

"And the car? Do you smoke in the car?"

"Yes."

The doctor scribbled in his notepad, thumb-clicked his pen, pocketed it, and told me that I could put my shirt back on. "Mrs. Schrand, considering Brandon's history of allergies and his asthma, I strongly recommend you and your husband change your smoking habits at once. He has difficulty breathing under the best conditions. Having to breathe in the constant presence of smoke is like, well, it's like breathing with a piano on your chest." I stared at my plaid pants and my Big Bird sneakers and imagined what it might be like to have a piano sitting on me.

Mom usually cracked the window when she smoked in the car, but that day, on the way home from the doctor's office, she rolled the window all the way down. After that, she stopped smoking in my bedroom too.

IV.
Seneca, the ancient tragedian, orator, and writer, also suffered from asthma. He noted that of all illnesses that had visited him, asthma was the most menacing. "One could hardly, after all, expect anyone to keep on drawing his last breath for long, could one? . . . This is why doctors have nicknamed it 'rehearsing death,' since sooner or later the breath does just what it has been trying to do all those times." But he did not acquiesce to the haunting "squall" of asthma. Instead, he defied it, dared it to take him while he was sleeping: "I shall not be afraid when the last hour comes." Unlike Seneca, I feared the last hour, entertained nightmares about the last hour, recurring ones that replayed the scene at my aunt Marcia's house.

V.
Air, it seems, is not easily won in my family. We lived in Richland, Washington, for only three years before Dad was laid off from Hanford, forcing us to vacate our white, two-bedroom clapboard rental and move back to Soda Springs. There, my grandparents owned an historic three-story brick hotel, café, and bar right downtown and had enlisted my parents to help run the place. It was a family business in the strictest sense, and we all lived there, squared away in apartments on the ground floor. Because my grandparents' apartment was larger, though, I lived with them.

A few years before my asthma attack, my grandfather was diagnosed with emphysema, and although he quit smoking his Winstons, he refused to go on oxygen. His doctor urged him, emphatically, to use it, supplementally, at least at night. It would help, he said. Afraid of becoming dependent upon a tank, afraid of that kind of entrapment, my grandfather dug in and tried to fight the disease. Inevitably, though, he lost ground as everyone knew he would. Drawing a full breath became more and more labored. By the time we moved back to Soda Springs, a cold green steel cylindrical tank filled with pure oxygen stood at the head of his bed. As a child, I was vaguely frightened of this armless gargoyle that towered in my grandparents' room. It looked like a beheaded soldier, a robot, or a bomb that could explode at any second.[4]

Only those patients who have advanced emphysema need supplemental oxygen, but all sufferers will need it eventually. The disease is particularly troubling because the lungs lose their elasticity. Those afflicted with emphysema are encumbered with the haunting reality that it is not just a progressively arduous task to draw a full breath, but it is inordinately difficult to exhale the breath once they have taken it.

My grandparents tried everything to outpace his degenerative respiratory condition. They tried steroids, exercise, inhalers, herbal remedies, prayer, anger, denial. At one point they drove to Mexico to look for large and inexpensive quantities of cortisone, a drug, they were told, offered relief for various victims. While some days were better than others, we all knew that eventually my grandfather's fears would come true: he would rely on an oxygen tank for the rest of his life. And that this disease would kill him.

If my grandpa smoked before he volunteered to fight in World War II, he smoked twice as much by the end of the war. There is little doubt that smoking led to and caused his disease. But for years after the war, his lungs saw no reprieve. He harvested grain on combines without

---

[4] An aside: When I was in elementary school, I formed a club based on Bertrand R. Brinley's children's books, *The Mad Scientists' Club*. The books centered on a smart but goofy cast of characters who hatched hair-brained ideas with intent to help their nostalgically named town of Mammoth Falls. Their plans and schemes always backfired, of course, but these "failures" did not deter them from trying other experiments. Fully taken by these stories, I started to hatch some schemes of my own. One involved building a rocket out of my grandpa's oxygen tank. I cobbled together a launchpad out of two pallets, four cinder blocks, and scrap lumber. On notebook paper, I sketched a number of designs and schematics. Each one, however, hinged on the same ignition theorem: the rocket would launch if I knocked the valve off the tank with a twenty-pound sledgehammer. It would have to be a clean strike. One hit. The fear of a spark and a certain explosion, however, distressed me greatly and caused many sleepless nights. The launch was canceled indefinitely. I don't think it ever occurred to me, though, that it would have been my grandfather's air I was shooting into the horizon, his part-time life support system that would have surely exploded in our driveway.

cab enclosures, mowing through thunderheads of splintery chaff and grain dust. And when he wasn't attending to the ranch, he worked at Monsanto where columns of smoke filled the sky and thickened the air.

VI.
Like Mom, who had stopped smoking in my bedroom when I was diagnosed with asthma, Grandma also quit smoking her Bel-Air Menthols in their bedroom when Grandpa was hit with emphysema. I will not soon forget the artwork that adorned her cigarette packages. A crisp blue windblown sky feathered with a light, airy wisp of a cloud. The very package was the image of the freshest air imaginable.

Best of all, the packages came with coupons that could be redeemed for merchandise from the company's glossy-slick catalog. Grandma collected the coupons and one summer, gave me two shoe boxes filled with rubber-banded bundles that I mailed off to the Raleigh Bel-Air company in exchange for a red Tasco telescope with a black tripod and a yellow-and-blue two-person inflatable rubber raft complete with oars and air pump.[5] Combined, the two items required over two thousand cigarette coupons. I was ecstatic. I raced my bike over the sidewalks to the post office daily to see if any large boxes awaited me. Day after day, I returned home winded and disappointed.

The day my raft and telescope arrived, however, marked the day I redoubled my efforts to collect more coupons. At night I lay in my bed beneath a large skylight and flipped through the merchandise catalog, my wish book. And five times an hour the skylight would glow orange, coloring, if only faintly, the glossy catalog pages I thumbed through and marked with a ballpoint pen. I circled the full-color pictures of binoculars, compasses, bicycles, watches, radios, a color TV Math problems—columns of addition and subtraction—riddled the margins.

---

[5] It is probably safe to say that few people today pay much attention to the common air-pump, but there was a time when its early incarnations generated a great deal of scientific discussion. The Honourable Robert Boyle, for instance, who is largely credited as the progenitor of modern chemists, was fascinated with the air pump. In 1657, he happened across an early model of the air pump—created by Otto Von Geuriecke, a German physicist who experimented with, among other things, vacuums and generators—and worked for two years on improving the contraption. And by 1659, Boyle had completed the new and improved "machina Boyleana," which led to a number of significant experiments on the properties of air. The common air pump was integral to those experiments.

So many coupons for the compass left only so many for the FM radio. Possibilities abounded. The cardboard carton that held my new batch of coupons was pathetically empty, however, so I pestered Grandma making certain that every coupon was accounted for. "How many packs did you smoke today, Grandma?" I would ask, beaming. It was our running joke. "I can only smoke so many a day, you know!" She would say, and laugh.

VII.

On bright afternoons, I visited with Grandpa in his bedroom. He had an adjustable bed that, when elevated, made it easier for him to draw and release his breath. Their bedroom had a large window and the two of us would sit on the edge of his bed, share a bowl of cherries, spit the stones into the waste basket, and talk on all matters of the world—whether or not ESP was real, would California sink in the big quake, would Russia launch a missile at the US, and would Soda Springs be a target? All the while his oxygen hissed in the background. Sometimes I set up my telescope in his room so I could look through his window. Once, while I dragged the lens across the horizon, my eye intent on anything and nothing (usually a stand of cottonwoods or a skein of geese over distant brushy hills), and while my fingers dialed the fine-focus knob, Grandpa popped me on the head playfully. I looked at him, blinking. I was standing on his oxygen hose. "Oh, sorry," I said. "I didn't know."

Asthma does not affect the tissues in the lungs like emphysema. Asthmatics struggle to breathe because the bronchi in their lungs narrow and restrict airflow. Many people who suffer from asthma rely on aerosol inhalers when they feel particularly short of breath, like I did when I wrestled in junior high school.[6] I remember the gymnasium where we practiced and how the air was heavy and humid and odor-

---

[6] During the composition of this essay, I came down with bronchitis, and was prescribed an inhaler in addition to the usual regimen of antibiotics. "Because of your history with asthma," the doctor said, regarding the inhaler. I checked the active ingredients for oxygen, but found none. Instead, I learned that the L-shaped canister contained a "microcrystanlline suspension of albuterol in propellants [trichloromonofluoromethane and dichlorodifluoromethane] with oleic acid." Whatever *that* is, you won't find it among Seven-Eleven Japan's chic assortment of canned oxygen.

ous, and how it hung like weather. Thin, smallish, and light on my feet, I could sprint as fast as anyone on the team, at least for the first half-dozen wall touches. Then the ceiling lights blurred yellow while my chest burned and I would invariably fall behind the rest of the team, gradually at first (I can still hear my coach, a balding man built like a meat locker: *Come on, Schrand! Pick it up!*), and finishing last, sucking the sour air. My lungs felt raw and shredded. I would stumble to the court's edge and snatch up my inhaler and blast its foul gas into my throat. I hated that inhaler, though, because it was viewed by my coach and teammates as a weakness, an excuse, somehow emasculating. As the corridors in my lungs closed in on themselves, I understood what it must be like to have someone stand on my oxygen hose.

VIII.
Seneca did not have an inhaler. Nor did asthmatics in the nineteenth century; rather, they had the West. They had places like Soda Springs, Idaho. My grandfather had Soda Springs, too, but one day decided that the air was better elsewhere than it was in his hometown. And just like that, without ceremony or explanation, he and my grandma packed their red Volkswagen Rabbit and drove into the desert southwest, and settled for the winter in Bullhead, Arizona. They moved not for the weather, but for the air—his fresh-air cure. "He just knew he could breathe better there," Grandma often says. "And what the hell? It was worth a shot."

My grandfather stopped breathing and died in a fluorescent-lit hospital room on the night of January 4, 1986. I was fourteen and remember clearly the moment he flatlined and how Mom ran out of the room, sobbing. I also remember not knowing how to react, so I didn't. I just remember the sound and Mom bolting, her face in her hands. And how the oxygen kept hissing long after he was gone.

It is summer. Almost twenty years have passed since my grandfather died. I sit in my grandmother's house and talk loudly because she is losing her hearing. My two children are not with me, so she smokes in the living room. When my wife and I visit and the kids are with us, Grandma retreats to her bedroom, shuts her door, and smokes quietly there, hidden away. Other times she will slip out the back door. When we stay over we pitch a tent in the backyard in the cool open air. My grandma doesn't mind. It relieves her some because she is hyper-conscious of her smoking. Four years ago she spent over one hundred dollars on an air purifier. The next year she bought another at nearly four hundred dollars. She cleans the filter obsessively while we are there. She asks us time and again, "Can you tell a difference? Does it seem better in here?" And time and again we nod eagerly and say *Oh, yes. My! A big difference!* In reality, though, we cannot detect a change at all. I still find it difficult to breathe in her house and everything smells like smoke. The furniture, walls, carpet, everything. I used to joke that even the tap water smelled like cigarette smoke. I often wonder if her air purifying contraption is as bunk as the Buena Ventura, if it might be this century's mythic "fresh air cure."

This time back though the mood is slightly strained. Her breathing, I've noticed, is labored and heavy, her coughing fits, violent. And although I notice for the first time that an inhaler sits on the kitchen counter near her glass ashtray, I say nothing. I ignore it because she does not want to talk about it. Earlier in the morning she had gone to the doctor and was told that she may very well have emphysema, but he wasn't certain.[7] To be certain, he sent her home with a monitor that would track the flow of oxygen in her bloodstream. She is supposed to use it at night. "They want to see if I need oxygen. What a bunch of crap." She is obstinate. "At my age? What the hell is the point?"

IX.

The mythology of the American West, which is an extension of the larger American mythology that begat it, goes like this: the land and the air and the watersheds and the species and everything down to a singular broom of spindly bog sedge, are ours. It has all been willed to us by some greater power, and it is all there for our taking. Manifest Destiny told us that the American West was the Garden of Eden all over again, a notion nineteenth-century travel writers like Horace Greeley, John Codman, and Clarence King promoted variously. To suggest that we have abandoned the garden mythology for a land-wise, water-wise,

---

[7] For reasons that aren't exactly clear, emphysema is more common in men than it is in women, a fact that offered some hope for my grandma's health.

air-wise ideology is foolhardy. Manifest Destiny still runs in our blood, and is the blank check that funds strip-mining, feedlots, and agri-giants. And mitigative measures such as reclamation do little to offset the consequences of our dominant mythologies. After all, reclamation presupposes that whatever is being reclaimed was ours to claim in the first place. We believe this mythology so entirely that we have created a federal agency—the Bureau of Reclamation—in its honor.

Evidence that threatens to unravel our garden mythology—that suggests that the pristine is polluted, that the virgin is penetrated, or that the Buena Ventura was imaginative—is very often met with denial, derision, or dismissiveness. Consider, for instance, a recent AP article about the air quality in Soda Springs: "People living in the area of Soda Springs . . . have a health risk score that is nearly 109 times higher than the national average for other neighborhood tracts included in the 2000 census. The Soda Springs census tract ranks 283rd out of the nation's 65,443 census tracts for the highest risk of industrial air pollution in the country."

The article cites the air in my hometown as the thirteenth most polluted in the nation. It also says that federal regulators point to two culprits behind this diseased air: Monsanto and Agrium, a local corporation that produces industrial amounts of fertilizer.

Three days after this article surfaced, I scanned this headline in the *Caribou County Sun*, my hometown's newspaper: "Monsanto Circulates Fact Sheet to Correct Health Risk Story." The "fact sheet" was released hours after the AP article appeared, and no one in Soda Springs questioned, at least publicly, the veracity of the document. Monsanto's message was clear and unwavering: *The AP article was absurd. It was flat wrong. Their data modeling methodology was botched; nothing could be further from the truth.*

I was troubled for any number of reasons. The intriguing way the paper framed the debate: the "fact sheet" correcting the "story." Monsanto's lightning-fast reaction. The sweeping assurances, the brio in their insistence. The fox insuring us the henhouse is shipshape, that Eden is still Eden, and that all is well.[8] But I was most troubled by what was not said, by the holes in the logic. The AP story, as they termed it, may very well have been flawed. The data could have been skewed. But this is hardly a yes-the-air-is-polluted, no-it's-not dilemma as Monsanto's fact sheet would have us believe. I am not a scientist, but I can say with some certainty that data sets—especially those dealing in parts per million—rarely work in absolutes, but rather gradations. Maybe the air in Soda Springs is not the thirteenth most industrially polluted in the nation, but could it be the sixteenth or seventeenth, or fifth for that matter? It is difficult to know. What is not difficult to know, however, is that the air in Soda Springs today is not the same elastic air John Codman once sought to relieve his asthma.

X.

It is commonly known that coal miners used to truck caged canaries into the mines as instruments that warned of imminent danger. The canaries' hypersensitive respiratory systems could detect a sudden shift in the air quality, and should the shaft fill with carbon monoxide, the canaries would tip over, giving the miners their short, albeit only, chance to evacuate.

On an already-hot morning in August of 1996, Scott Dominguez, an old high school friend of mine, did not have such a chance to evacuate. He had gone to work that morning, like he did every morning, at Evergreen Resources, Inc., a Soda Springs company that converted mining by-product trucked in from Kerr-McGee (another local operation) into fertilizer. That morning, Scott's boss, Allen Elias—an industrial tycoon infamous for violating multiple environmental safeguards—ordered Scott to clean the sludge out of the bottom of a twenty-five thousand gallon tank. Elias sent Scott into the tank without protective clothing, and when Scott asked for a respirator, his boss seethed: "There's nothing in that tank but mud and water. It's as safe as ordinary shampoo."

Fearful of losing his job, Scott descended into the darkness of the tank. Armed with nothing but a fire hose and broom, Scott went to work. But it wasn't long before he knew something was wrong. By the

---

[8] Monsanto is not beyond reproach in the arena of environmental matters. For over four decades they knowingly saturated the small town of Anniston, Alabama, with PCBs (carcinogenic industrial coolants) by unloading "millions of pounds" of the waste into landfills and streams. They were sued and fined seven hundred million dollars in human and ecological damages. Anniston is now virtually uninhabitable as a result of the contamination.

time two of his co-workers started yelling down into the tank, Scott had already pitched face-first into the gray sludge. An ordinary canary would have been dead once it was lowered into the tank because it was filled with hydrogen cyanide gas. Scott suffered irreparable brain and physical damage. The EPA launched an investigation into Evergreen Resources, and the case climbed to the US Supreme Court. Now Elias sits in a Texas prison and Scott struggles day to day with speech and motor skills.

I cannot pass over the haunting irony of Evergreen as the name of a company that converted waste into fertilizer and nearly killed its employees in the process. If there were ever an ideological disconnect between our mythology and the results of that mythology, Evergreen Resources might typify it. Doesn't the name "Evergreen" connote notions of perpetuity and fecundity? Couldn't the company also be called The Perpetual Garden? Maybe so. Another example of this disconnect is shown in a recent Kerr-McGee television commercial. It shows a mountain desert brushed with fields of snow. A Bel-Air blue sky. Wild horses thunder across the open space and then slow, stop, and nudge what is presumably a natural gas plant. The assuring voice-over—set against some faintly patriotic background music—talks of fuel exploration (mining) and wild nature (streams, meadows, air) existing as one, not as strange bedfellows but as lovers. The machine courting the garden.

XI.
We need the miner's canary as metaphor. We need it for the short term. The warning. The alarm system telling us that the air is no longer air, that night has become day, and that the Great Buena Ventura runs not through Utah's west desert, but through Eden, and that its headwaters are found in our imaginative dreams. What is most important though is that we find a canary for the long term, one whose respiratory system is hypersensitive to changes that can and will occur hundreds of years from now. We need a metaphor that will free us from our indenture to mythology. But as long as we can walk to our faucets and expect water, and as long as we can trust cigarette packages and fact sheets, Monsanto, Hanford, and Evergreen, and as long as we can step outside and expect the air to be there, pure and bracing, the mythology will march on with real consequences hanging in the balance.

ohio from the fleeting
Gabrielle Jesiolowski

we followed railroad tracks, divinations, canal ways leading away
from the highways

ohio   usually the grave rubbings or low sheds first into sight & as a
child i did not learn
to paint   my mother drew the spine of an urchin

from ohio you lose your body   the memory of hands becomes a collective memory
hidden inside the organs of churches:
        the boy would fast and rarely come out from behind
the organ
another choked himself between the wood slats of the pavilion

    quiet was invaded with trumpets dragged through the earth,
that kind of a sound
would keep you up
ohio

        it was a tornado that never touched but slowly eyed
the land
        walking through corn for deities, for cities

Kinderszenen
William Reichard

(Scenes from childhood, after Robert Schumann)

One

There is never enough money. There is never enough to eat. When there is enough to eat, there is never enough of our mother because someone has to work. My father rarely works. My father works at being crazy. Being crazy is a lot of work. Being crazy requires a great deal of money. There is never enough money. There is never enough to eat.

Two

I collect seeds in a jar. This is the year of the near foreclosure, the year of the second fake heart attack. My father grabs at his chest and rolls around on the floor. My sisters scream. I don't know about it, being with my brother down the street when it happens. The ambulance comes, sirens screaming. We wonder who died, then continue to play. My father convalesces. Being crazy is a lot of work; it takes practice to make your heart race. My father is fired from his job. My mother takes a job at a factory. The factory prints magazines and catalogs. My mother works the night shift. My father doesn't work at all. During the day, my mother does housework At night, she makes catalogs and magazines. She never earns enough money. We never see her.

Three

We lose a piano. We lose some guns. We lose our minibikes. We lose our car. Things in this universe never vanish, but change, change form, change hands. Other hands now hold our things and we are going hungry. The bank asks for the house back. My mother panics. My father naps. Thinking we'll have to leave our house, I walk around the yard and collect seeds from each plant there. I put them in jars. I think I can plant them in whatever new house we move to. Someone else's house, maybe. A house stolen from other hands. When it becomes clear that we will not move, I take the jar of seeds and stow it in the crawl space under my bedroom floor. I leave it there. Years later, my mother moves to a smaller house. I forget the seeds.

Four

Our family cat is my best friend. I play with hollyhocks, hide in tall grass in the big ditch along the highway. One day, two cars crash. Blood and glass everywhere. People flood the road. Police swarm. Onlookers trample our garden to get a better view. Through a shattered windshield, a man's face, trapped inside the car. His skull has taken a new shape. Sirens slice the summer air. Welders cut the cars apart but it's too slow a process. The face collapses. From my vantage point in the strawberry patch, I watch the man die.

Five

Steady breath. Steady breath. Steady breath. Pedaling up the hill near Rathaie's pasture. Pedaling past the cows. Crows perched on phone lines. The sun unbearable. My skin brown and burning. Steady breath. The scent of freshly cut alfalfa makes my mouth water. Remember the taste of honeysuckle juice, the taste of raw sweet corn stolen from neighboring fields. August's heat. The swamp drawn down by drought; the turtles resting in the sun; the dogs that chase from the lonely driveways of small farms. Steady breath. Pedaling. Getting somewhere.

Six

Another one gone. A ceremony in a small town, in a courthouse. A rare dress, my mother in tears and nice lady shoes. A cake. A keg. A drunken husband. A room now empty. A sister married. Another one gone.

Seven

Constant chatter from the canary my mother keeps because her mother always kept one. My grandmother's birds lived. My mother's die, one by one, small yellow corpses and a trip to the backyard where my best friend the cat lies buried. Add a canary. Plant a tree. My mother tries to live as she was taught. The cannas brought from Nebraska, from her mother's garden, grow bold and scatter around the garden in no particular order. Constant chatter from the canary as my father smokes in the dining room, the room where the bird's cage hangs. The chatter subsides in a gray smoky tide. My sister Linda coughs. The bird dies. The matches are struck, one by one. They flare. My father coughs.

Eight
I collect books. I steal books. I buy books. I borrow books. I bury myself in words.

Nine
We try to build a fort. My brother Andy cuts his hand on rusty tin. Blood everywhere. The fort is abandoned but the tin still stands, still nailed to a tree, thirty years later.

Ten
No one cries when he leaves. No one dies of heartbreak. I've seen this in the movies. He packs his things in plastic bags and goes off coughing in a powder blue Buick with power windows and power seats and lives at my sister Wanda's house, three and a half miles away. It seems like infinity, the distance we span. No one cries when he's gone. No one misses him.

Eleven
Across the chalk outline of my hand on the sidewalk, a small cat stands. Brown. Dull. Crabby. He crosses the line. The one where I've said "no." He comes over anyway. We take him in.

Twelve
There is never enough money. There is never enough to eat. Nights, I sit in my room and read. Days, I sleep through school, too tired to read. Weekends, I drink or ride my bike
    steady breath, steady breath, steady breath
                              always pedaling.
My cat Max sits on my lap. Always moving. Dreaming. A book open to a particular page. A dictionary dealing out definitions. There is never enough money. There is never enough to eat. I find I am always hungry. I read in a book how it is accomplished. I look at a map. Then I get ready to go there.

Thirteen

The night I find *Swan Lake* on television, the broadcast is grainy on a black and white set. How he, the Prince, moves! How she, the cursed Princess, dances! How can you believe in something you never knew existed? The wonder of motion, arms as wings. How the wind across the prairie tricks us into belief. How the soul conspires, at last, to throw us into a world where we belong, to startle us awake, into paradise.

No Motive
LUANNE DIBERNARDO

There was nothing more she could do and so that's what she did, nothing. Variations of it, like the nothing of watching television, her eyes blinking themselves across the room like a fly in search of a worthy landing, hopeless. The nothing of walking past bedrooms that refused to feel empty, the air still fattened with anguish. The nothing of laundering clothes, of dusting furniture, the nothing of feeding herself when hungry or not, her pangs unnoticed for years now. The nothing of washing her face, of walking the hall where she never noticed the threadbare path insisting she search for something since gone, where nobody waited to be stretched, wiped, or bathed in a room where nothing, not anything, remained to be done, to the couch where if she rested or not it just wouldn't matter.

Irene would be sixty-seven in about as many days, a number she hadn't given thought to until filling out her sons' admission forms, Conor and Kirk, forty-four-year-old twins with the same ruddy freckles, same crimson curls, even the same degenerative disease, two who lived longer than anyone reasoned, not her words. She barely noticed their abilities lessen, her duties multiply since they turned nineteen, twenty-one years of caretaking, no use to think about how or if she might manage one more hour, one more year, not so much as one moment's thought to her own deterioration, or to the possibility that her children's lives might have been any different, her own life an afterthought.

Her calendar crossed nine months since her boys had been moved, nine months that Forest Lakes Nursing Home had been doing what she had done for so many years, at least until the seizures grew closer, their heads bent low like swans left sleeping. Food moved through feeding tubes and through to their veins, while beneath the boys' beds hung bladders of urine, emptied now by nurses and not their mother, though she visits them daily. Daily, though there's nothing, not one thing left that Irene can do, and so she does what she does.

The gun she takes from what was once her husband's dresser, the only drawer unchanged these twenty-three years since his unexpected death. Her hands move to touch his short-sleeved T-shirts, reluctant to waken their hope. Her fingers, precise in their movements, disappear between the folded shirts then return without pause, the pistol not nearly as frightening as the injectors she used to stab her sons' buttocks, the next day their thighs, always one blackening, always one yellowing. The gun in her hand looks small and uncomplicated, easier to use than the pulleys and lifts that inhabit her home. Irene finds herself drawn by the size of the bullets, how small and good they feel in her hand, how beautifully they slide into each perfect chamber, if only a catheter found a bladder as well. She loads five chambers because five are empty, finds herself moved by the few left in her hand, like sea glass, smooth and cool.

Sea glass, she muses, when in the same manner an ear can pop clear, her mind gives way to a minuscule crack, a jagged rupture that dares to expose what long lay buried. A crack so devastatingly clear that, for a moment, Irene is staring at something unbearable, a sensation more real than the pleasing weight of her husband's gun pressed into her lap, against her groin. She sees him, her then-alive husband on somebody's motorcycle, a self-proclaimed freebird like Kirk, with his basketball, his August flirtations. Irene watches, cannot look away from her husband's back, his body less muscle than movement, his forearms stretched forward to clutch the bike's handles, his movements motored by impulse, desire. His smile unmatched, unforgettable, though somehow she had managed. Their sons, one like him, one like her, wait on the beach, their skinny legs bent beneath them like hinges for raising them close to, then down from, their castles of sand. Through this unforeseen crack, Irene watches closely their boyish arms, how they move the way boyish arms are meant to, unknowingly; how, she wonders, could she ever have looked away? For this moment she sees what she didn't see then, how the pale brown sand catches light against Kirk's damp thighs, against the blades of her boys' young wings, daintily dusted with gold from their hole dug to China.

Irene sees it all with microscopic clarity. The sun, selfish when it steals behind clouds leaving nothing for cover, the boys uncaring, she shivers, they stay. She feels what she is certain she didn't feel then, the cold, cruel drips from her heavy, dark hair (how, unwilling to forget, it held the lake). The pull of her skin slowly drying, her breasts shrunken firm and away from the cups of her cold, damp swimsuit, the close, fine hairs of her face tickling free from bondage, the absolute christening of sun, of wind, on her wet and naked skin. She takes in the lake with painful remembrance, how it roars in rhythmic crescendos, urgent rushes that deafen what might be heard, the ingenuous likelihood of a motorcycle returning, unbearable to now recall.

It is with thoughts from those places that Irene recalls her sons in their nursing home suite, fire- and sun-proof curtains behind them, worn linoleum their feet never met, that smell. Where nurses steal time to swathe their prickled skin or wheel them to the Activity Room where more able patients will do what they can, where Conor and Kirk will do nothing, their torsos strapped to the back of their chairs. Their minds, she prayed, were staled or calcified, inconceivable to think they might be aware of even one moment, or worse, that through some jagged crack of their own, they might, like her, remember.

It is with thoughts from those places that Irene gets up from the blond veneer bed that was meant to be temporary, a loan from Kirk's mother their first year of marriage. Beside it, a wooden dresser with wooden knobs she always meant to replace with pulleys of iron or faceted glass. Over the dresser stares a square mirror with its years of brazen judgments, until now, she thinks while noticing not the way it reflects, but rather how it condones her movements, to the point she almost considers looking back before moving away from the temporary scape of dresser, bed, and mirror, a room she knew well, completely unchanged into something she barely recognized.

It is with thoughts from those places that Irene leaves her house and drives the seven miles that still feel foreign, her hands on the wheel of a car passing buildings she's never entered, past trees never seen, past streets not yet paved. Past corner after corner of look-alike marts built for last-minute pleasures. She stops for lights at intersections that only serve to stall her progress, though for once she isn't rushing.

It is with thoughts from those places she enters the nursing home lobby, to the pasteled paintings of seascapes, of seagulls, to the Maalox-pink drapes, the peach-flavored walls that left her more queasy than chemo, the treatments she took in a room of paisley, with skylights, with floor lamps instead of fluorescents, with music and plants and magazines that haven't already expired, a room for the living. Treatments that asked less than thirty minutes, a selfish hal-hour with doctors who nodded to nurses who stopped for a smile. To her they spoke of an end in sight, her guilt eased only when doubled with pain, her ribs left weak, her penance renewed with each convulsion, her conscience clear for one more night.

These months later, Irene passes through her sons' benign lobby, her body renewed by remission, not her words. For once she hears nothing—not Agnes's tormented pleading, or beyond the nurses' station, not Olive who cries for her mother, or Buddy who warbles "The Tennessee Waltz" from one of many misaligned wheelchairs. Not Mary, who hails garçon! to anyone boarding her cruise ship, if only a ruse for Irene's two sons.

She passes them all, each foot grounded, flat as permanence. If asked, she would say that she had no thoughts, no mind left to know what allowed her to act in ways a mother should never—to prick and poke the flesh she bore, to pipeline fluids from paralyzed organs, to mimic movement despite limbs numbed by atrophy. She would say that she had no thoughts at all, too ashamed to acknowledge all she recalled from the lake, the remembered caress of leftover sand mixed with evening's damp sheets on their sunburned skin. No mind for thinking about what she does next, just one foot in front of the other until she passes the fire extinguisher that signals the bend towards Kurt and Conor's room.

She approaches the skirt of her sons' doorless entry—inside, two boys, never men, now strangers. Her hand moves the way her feet once moved, on their own, a necessary function, and so effortless as she aims for the head that was Conor's, not one moment's pause before sighting the head that was Kirk's. She waits and she watches, uncertain, their bodies unchanged by what she has done, as if nothing at all just happened. Only that blood flows freely from both boys' heads, for once not out through a needled vein, for once not pressured into a vial, their blood long tired, futile.

As if nothing at all just happened, she turns from the still-pumping pumps and the still-breathing tanks, away from their room and back down the hall past the fire extinguisher. Nothing, as she passes through the stagnant air, through Agnes's chant, "Help me, help me, Mr. Odairs, Christopher Robin is saying his prayers," to whomever might listen. Not Irene, who returns to the pale peach lobby where she sits and waits, for the first time unafraid, for the first time not guilty for what she has done. Somewhere in the distance the wail of sirens screaming for someone who waits for their arrival, finally not Conor, not Kirk, though her body remembers to stiffen, Irene unaware. Unaware how her hand still wraps the graceful machine that responded each time, her fingers still clenched as if her life depended on it.

Across the Street
Jean Esteve

In suits and ties and hats and hose
they file inside their bright new walls.
All those sinners, all their sins
so amiably combined within.

A piercing shadow falls across
the Sunday funnies on my porch.
Fuckers, move your goddamned church,
it's cutting off my reading light.

Whole Hog
Tenaya Darlington

Three seasons out of the year, I don't see my next-door neighbor Kim. Just traces of him—the trail of his cigarette, the sound of his Harley each morning at first light, and sometimes at night, the blue glow of his hot tub, which materializes out of the Wisconsin darkness like a ghostly window of sky. A quiet guy, he rarely appears at neighborhood gatherings—the winter solstice potluck, the Day of the Dead fête, the annual thirty-seventh birthday party of my neighbor Cherie, which inevitably turns into an all-night extravaganza of daiquiris and Sufi dancing and dogs dressed in little costumes. Kim is an auto mechanic, a stout, bearded man in his sixties who has lived in the same house since he was fifteen. Nine months out of twelve, he stores up his burly gusto for the one party he throws each year: his summer pig roast.

Kim is a summer lover. More than anyone in our neighborhood (affectionately referred to as "the massage ghetto," for its surplus of body workers), he knows how to maximize his warm-weather pleasure. A few years back, he installed a beer tap next to his sliding screen door so he could pour a cold one from his deck without having to leave his lawn chair. Before that, he installed a platform for his television across from the Jacuzzi, so he could watch the Packers games while submerged. On Sundays, his bearded face and pint glass are barely visible above the blue foam.

In downtown Madison, where the yards are narrow and the trees are thin, Kim is the ultimate urban outdoorsman, and nothing—not his deck, not his canoe, not his mysterious spelunking gear in the garage—showcases his talent for masterminding a bona fide summer blowout like his pig roast. Three years running, it features a different porcine personality each time around with posters that precede the event, announcing the coming of "Willy the Pig" or "Harry the Hog" until a whole persona has evolved long before the poor thing arrives from pasture packed in ice.

As with many ritualistic events, there is an element of joyous crudeness to it, evident in the numerous drunken snapshots that have survived from past years, in which Kim and his grown son Roger pose with the Pig of the Year before it's cooked. In the photographs, Kim and his son hold up drafts of Budweiser, huge grins slashed across their beards. The pig, propped up on cinder blocks with an apple in its mouth, always sports the latest summer fashion: sunglasses, fishing hat, Hawaiian shirt. During the last election year, I seem to remember an American flag poking up through a hoof.

It takes two full days to slow-roast the pig. The job demands sentries, timers, someone with the stamina to make it through a night shift. Every fifteen minutes, coals must be carefully laid under the pig's sizzling body. The coals must be kept red hot, requiring careful watch over a set of hibachis stationed by Kim's garage. The whole process involves beer and fire, beer and fire. Through this, the neighborhood spirit is revived.

On the day the pig arrives, our block comes alive with both curiosity and revulsion. My neighbor Dana saunters down in a muumuu, carrying her requisite cup of sake, and stands against the fence across from the pig, imagining—despite her Jewish heritage—the forbidden taste of its sweetness. Behind her, the vegans gawk from their lawn, keen noses set to the west—*What is that smell? Oh Gawd*. And off they march in the opposite direction toward the grocery co-op, their vegan dog loping behind.

By late afternoon, a distinctly porcine smell begins to drift through my window screens. It's a smell unlike any other that wafts through our neighborhood—a place that is downwind from a coal plant with four smoke stacks that breathe constant black wisps into us. The smell of pig is stronger than that smell or the pungent smell of the lake that off-gases three blocks over or the bus exhaust from the busy street two blocks the other direction. It's sweet and smoky and utterly unlike the usual kitchen cross-breezes in our neighborhood, where tofu vindaloo and bulgur chili are *de rigueur*. It's a smell that's unavoidable as meat—big meat—and it penetrates everything. Leave your underwear drawer open during pig roast weekend and all your bras will smell like jerky.

By nightfall, a crew has assembled on Kim's dark deck and in the small patch of lawn opposite the roasting pit. Toddlers circle on tricycles. Adults lean on car hoods, bumming smokes—neighbors who aren't even smokers but who want to participate in the burning. The whole affair is testament to the power of fire, our innate attraction to it, the strange sense of community it awakens.

Across the street, the home-schooled teen buckles his bike helmet below his chin and rides off to dig through dumpsters without so much as a nod in our direction. His mother, sipping wine, says, "Meat has never passed his lips." It's hard to tell if the low tone of her voice comes from reverence or her own guilty pleasure.

On our street, where the masseuses are thick around us preaching good health and wholesome habits, food is political. The thought of going next door to borrow an egg or a cup of milk can set one in a quandary. Which house has gone lactose-free vegan? Is the yogi in the orange house fasting? While one person is getting off gluten, the next person is eating for O-negative. Diet, it seems, is as studied as the weather.

Just knowing that someone might have peered into your fridge while you were on vacation can feel more like a personal affront than if they'd gone through your bedside drawers. *I hope they didn't see the processed cheese singles in the meat drawer. Oh God, did I leave out the veal bratwurst?*

Oscar Mayer, which is busy pumping hot dogs into trucks less than five miles away, has probably never sold a Lunchable to anyone on our street, except maybe to Kim. Most neighbors shop at the nearby natural foods co-op, including myself. In fact, the co-op was one of the selling points when the realtor first showed me our little house. *Hardwood floors and we're only two blocks from an organic juice bar? Screw the gutted shower and the pentagrams in the basement, we'll take it!*

Although I'm the first person to support fine things like sustainable agriculture and raw milk cheese, I also recognize that the crusade for a whole foods diet has become a class issue. It requires leisure time to cook with kamut. It flat-out costs more to buy organic bananas. So, while I feel fortunate that I can buy Soysage around the corner, I secretly revel in the fact that my neighbor Kim roasts a pig each summer in what is basically my side yard. In this neighborhood, being a meat-and-potatoes man makes Kim the anomaly.

I grew up with barbecues and pig roasts in my home state of Iowa, as did my husband, who was raised in southern Indiana—a place where the sight of a giant barrel grill going down the highway was a sure sign of someone's shotgun wedding. When we return to our respective homes to visit relatives, meat on the table is still a given, and the process of getting meat on the table usually justifies a party, some social interaction involving small talk and spatulas and malt grain beverages.

Meat may be murder, but it's also Midwestern culture.

After sundown, when the pig is just beginning to spit after a full day on the coals, the guy who ritually does the night shift arrives: Kim's close friend Tim, a hunchbacked Vietnam vet. Tim, who drives a cab, usually pulls up in a taxi, a cigarette dangling from his lip, a six-pack in his lap. When he turns the car off and steps out, he'll head for the deck and pour himself a tall cold one from the tapper by the screen door, then settle in for his long night. Pacing and stoking. Pacing and stoking. The six-pack, he'll tell you, is just backup.

Tim's presence is also evidence of what the pig roast symbolizes—not necessarily to me or to the other neighbors, but to two men who go way back as beer-guzzling, euchre-playing guys who found each other when they lost their wives. The pig roast is the way Kim and Tim stoke their friendship. It's something they host together now, like a big family supper, Tim quietly smoking in a corner of the lawn while Kim serves up the beast.

I've seen marriages practically come to an end at the pig roast. One year, a husband and wife in their late forties—both long-time vegetarians—arrived together, poured themselves beers, and pulled up lawn chairs on opposite sides of the drive. They joined separate conversations, as any couple might, and made frequent trips to the card-table buffet where there was standard pig roast fare: vats of cole slaw, buckets of yellow potato salad, fruit cocktail studded with mini marshmallows. At some point, I noticed the vegetarian wife staring at her vegetarian husband. She fixated on him with a stony glare. Through the dusk, I squinted to see what he held in his hand, and by God, if it wasn't a pork sandwich.

It's hard to blame even the most devout vegetarian for sneaking a bite. There's a strange attraction to big meat, especially when you've smelled it cooking for hours upon hours. As repulsive as it may seem, its slow-cooked haunches crackle and glisten, and no one can listen long to the moans of satisfied diners without trying just a little piece.

Kim serves his roast pig the way Midwesterners serve group meat: sandwiched between slabs of cheap white bread with a glurp of barbecue sauce. If doughy wads of sandwich don't stick to the roof of your mouth, something's amiss.

I like to eat it unadorned, standing up, without a plate. Instead of a napkin, I like to wipe my greasy hands in the grass. Don't ask me why. In an urban setting, it's the closest I can get to camping, the same way that for Kim, roasting a pig in his tiny patch of yard is maybe the closest he can get to hunting or trapping. In this way, we are joined.

Most years, the pig roast has an ugly ending. Maybe that's the nature of a pig roast—it illuminates both the best and worst parts of civilization, a combination of reverence and cruelty. Usually, there is a drunken brawl, which isn't all that unusual on our street. Despite being the city's politically correct epicenter, there have been recent stabbings, police chases, muggings, drug raids. Suffice it to say, the pig roast draws in all kinds, including the local biker gang, the CC Riders. I know the meat is about to fall off the bore when I hear the sound of their Harleys.

The worst brawl came after Pig Roast II, year of Willy, I believe. I awoke late in the night to the sound of women shrieking in the street. Got up and peered out the bedroom window, where I could see Kim's deck, the hot tub full of pale bodies and blue light. In the drive, surrounded by burning torches, were two women, one of whom I recognized as my neighbor Renata from her motorized wheel chair. The other was Anne, a very poised black woman from the end of the block. Now, in some neighborhoods, people go to war over lawn care and unmindful pets, but in this neighborhood fights tend to get existential. Renata and Anne were arguing about the origins of slavery.

"Go home," I heard Kim holler from the tub. "Party's over, the food's all gone."

"Your people sold my people!" Anne kept insisting.

"I—am—the—liberator!" I heard Renata cry, not like a battle cry, but like a pressure valve releasing. Renata was not just tipsy, she was feeling utterly at one with the world despite the polarized feel of the neighborhood at that moment—made all the more spooky by the floating bodies, the burning torches. The two women kept their accusations going all the way down the block until their voices trailed off, the hum of Renata's motorized cart gradually blending in with the crickets.

That night I sat up in bed and stared at the ceiling fan's dim blur, waiting for the din next door to die down and thinking how strange it was to be at the apex of so many clashing cultures, how politicized our lives are, and how rarely so many kinds of people—meat eaters and non-meat eaters, academics and Harley riders, blacks and whites, Christians and Jews—sit down on the same curb to share a meal. To me, that's the best kind of neighborhood, a genuine melting pot. A true neighborhood bash should involve dialogue, darkness, something slow-roasted that leads to an unleashing of energies. It takes a certain kind of host to pull that off, someone fearless and without enmity, someone willing to put forth a sacrifice.

Last summer, I left the neighborhood. Kim moved out before I did—quit his day job, bought a biker bar in a small town not far from Madison. I also left to make a career change, and though it's been mostly positive, I still wake up in my apartment just outside Philadelphia and wonder where I am. I don't know anyone who eats Soysage here, and I never hear the sound of a Harley. As for body workers and yogis, they're completely priced out of this neighborhood.

Out my front window, I see a neatly arranged world, full of wide yards and primroses, mossy roofs and neatly swept drives. Predictable. Exclusive. I suppose in Kim's world, everything's coming up beer and Harley's—predictable, too, in its own way. Some might even argue exclusive. Although Kim and I have lost touch, I feel something missing there. I long for the nights leading up to the pig roast, for the sight of the hot tub winking on outside my window, for Tim stepping out of his car—even for the inevitable friction between certain neighbors.

During the pig roast, there was a mood in the air I have never found anywhere else. A feeling of impropriety versus propriety. A feeling of political versus personal. These tensions taught us to be tolerant neighbors, taught us to explore the unknown, and turned our homes into more than just boxes with flickering front windows. I suspect the mood I picked up on the night of pig roast is the same mood that's palpable right before a border crossing, when people who do not belong somewhere are about to set out for a new country. What they feel is, I'm guessing, a mix of brazenness and breathlessness, their very ethos brushing against a chasm. And the only way to make it is to venture forth wholeheartedly and with unabashed hunger.

Varieties of Loudness in Chicago
Elizabeth Crane

Paolo Pagano Jr. aspires to be louder. It runs in the family. Little Paulie, as he's known, is the loudest. Loudness is to this family what college is to others. It's their pride, and it's what they're good at.

Jennie Watson is almost as loud.

Paulie Pagano and Jennie Watson live approximately one hundred yards apart, separated by one building, one alley, a universe, and you.

The stabbing couple, two porches down, is close behind, but that's a story for later.

Jennie lives in the new condo across the street, a warehouse rehabbed into *a unique urban loft-style experience*. Paulie lives next door in a single-family home with his mother, who has, in her small parcel of land, an impressive vegetable garden. You won't be invited anytime soon, them not really knowing who you are, but you guess that a meal with the Paganos would be both interesting and delicious. You have never seen Paulie's mother smile, and suspect that it's been a long time. When she talks to the neighbors (a group with a surprising number of tenants who show some indications of being one family, although after several years of observation, you're still not sure), they connect by complaining over the fence. *My back*, Paulie's mother will say in her thick Italian accent. *The weather. My son.* The neighbors nod solemnly. They know about backs and weather and sons. *Your tomatoes are gorgeous,* they will say. These are people who traded in their grass for cement. *Too much trouble,* they had told Paulie's mother, who nodded solemnly. Miscellaneous other people are also in apparent residence at the Paganos'. These might include his sister, a girl who looks like his sister, and a heavyset guy who might be a cousin, but they're all frequently seen in the adjacent yard, so you can't be sure which sister belongs to which house. The girls who might be his sisters are also given toward loudness, although they aren't as ubiquitous and therefore appear somewhat less invested in their loudness than their possible brother. The girls who might be his sisters look just like Paulie, except they wear their hair in tight, shiny ponytails. These ponytails look like they could only hurt.

Jennie, in any case, likely has no such aspirations of loudness. She just is.

Little Paulie is twenty-three years old. When you moved in, he was seventeen and already bald. Upon hearing the news of his being a teenager, you spent some time examining him from your porch window whenever possible, trying to process this information, trying to understand how a seventeen-year-old anywhere could pass for forty, trying to understand what in seventeen years adds up to bald and forty-looking. You will come to know that possibilities include a dead dad and a close association with a bunch of local gangbangers, also loud, and who have no interest whatsoever in Paulie's front door, or any parts on or adjacent to it that might ring in a pleasant way, a way that only its occupants might hear. When they want to see Paulie, they come through the alley, and they yell *Paul-ee. Paul-ee!* Paulie never comes on the first eight or nine *Paulie*s. Usually his mother will intervene with a few more *Paulie*s, a final loud *Paolo!* and some words in Italian. She is a small, square woman, but you sense that she can and has and will again hit him and it will hurt. Little Paulie has one expression. It's a scowl.

Jennie, blonde, is twenty-six, a size four, and owns a clothing business and her condo, directly across from your front window. How you know this is she spends a good deal of time on her balcony (actually, it is more or less a railing in front of a set of sliding doors, with a plank just wide enough for one Jennie-sized person to stand on) talking on the phone and telling people these things. Jennie used to be a size two, but then she started working out. So she didn't *like, gain weight or anything,* her body *just totally changed which is a total bummer because I had like four pairs of Chip and Peppers and now I can't wear them at all.* Chip and Peppers are jeans that cost two hundred dollars. How you know this is she told the person she was talking to, who didn't know either. Jennie has several expressions, but they're all in the ballpark of overstimulated.

Paulie's interests include sitting on the roof of his garage, cars from the late seventies/early eighties, motorcycles, dogs, tattoos, rap, weed, and the sound of his own name. Sometimes these interests are combined in various ways to produce greater loudness. You suppose he wishes his dog were louder, but he's not much of a barker. Once he even tried to lick your hand, but Paulie yanked him back, clearly disappointed with the friendliness of his pitbull. Sometimes an afternoon will include a combination of rap played from the car (parked in the alley but running), weed, and some of the guys on the roof of his garage. On these days you stay off the porch. Paulie could pass you the joint from there. It would be uncomfortable.

Jennie's interests include Jennie. Or talking about Jennie. Boys and fashion, occasionally, but only as they pertain to Jennie. She's the kind of girl who will stop you in the middle of a story and say *that reminds me* and tell you a story about herself that has nothing to do with your story in any way you can discern. Your story could be about your sick aunt which will remind her of her aunt which will remind her of something about herself and your sick aunt will be no part of it.

When you first moved in, you could tell it was summer when the scent of night-blooming jasmine filled the air and the neighborhood kids started shooting. The storage warehouse across the street was largely quiet except on nights when the neighborhood kids hung around, sometimes with babies in tow, fighting about who'd been in the neighborhood longer, interesting in no small part due to the fact that the people fighting about this topic were barely fourteen. You'd moved in that week and you'd been there longer. In spite of her own short time there, Jennie has her own proprietary feelings about her corner of the street. She will talk to anyone who is moving in, looking in, and it seems, merely walking by, and tell them that she was the first one to move in. You have the sense that in a certain way she believes she's pioneered the very concept of moving. What interests you here is that every word uttered by Jennie is distinctly audible but never can you hear the person she's talking to. Or at. You have the sense that Jennie thinks of herself and her living here as *edgy*. Whatever this means, though, she isn't. You aren't even edgy, and you were here before the condos came. You live here because it's cheap, but it's worth noting that you feel at ease here in a way you never do on the Gold Coast. On the Gold Coast you feel like an impostor.

The summer Jennie moves in is also the summer of the motorcycle. Little Paulie gets a bike and rides it often but always comes back within ten minutes. You are fairly sure that Paulie removed the muffler upon purchase, and that he comes back quickly because he will not go farther than can be heard in his own hood. That there would be no point if his loudness were heard only by strangers. Kind of like if a tree falls in the forest, if the tree cares whether or not the forest hears it make a sound. You believe that if for some reason his license were revoked, that Paulie would be just as happy to gun the bike in back of his house. You have seen him ride from the alley to the corner deli, which might be twenty paces from his front door. But as you know, Paulie does not use the front door in any capacity, answering, entering, or exiting, and perhaps Paulie is thinking that someone will think he came from somewhere else.

Jennie walks to the deli, but prefers to hold her fights in the street. For a while, she has a boyfriend. He has highlights in his flat-ironed hair. This isn't what they fight about. This is what they have in common. What they fight about is him not paying enough attention to her feelings. *How could you not know that my ex–best friend wore that horrible perfume and that it would bring back terrible feelings?* Jennie has her arms spread wide and her head forward. If she weren't a size four it might be a threatening posture. What it seems like coming from Jennie is something she saw someone do on that *Laguna Beach* show. *It was a gift! I can't read your fucking mind!* he shouts. *And I'm sick of fucking trying. I never asked you to!* Jennie yells. *I told you what I wanted! Okay,* he says, *then I'm sick of you. And I'm gone. Whatever!* she shouts, turning back to her apartment. You sense that she can and has and will again, if he comes back, hit him. Fights like this tend to take place after you've gone to bed but are worth getting up for. Sometimes you even go watch the show with your downstairs neighbor. He's always up late. Later, you will find out that Jennie and her boyfriend have broken up five times already since they met three months prior. *I'm so sure he'll be back,* she says, having wasted no time getting on the phone. You're so sure that if he does, she will hit him. But it won't hurt, which will only make him look like more of a wuss.

Rumors have gone around about Paolo Pagano Sr., that he was a small time mob guy, that he was rubbed out or whacked or whatever they say, but that Little Paulie didn't show a lot of promise in the area of Mafia, and so was overlooked when time came to promote. Paulie compensates for this by going to jail anyway. You will never know why for sure; you will only know that this is the quietest summer ever on your block. You know only that one day when you hear a gunshot, you look out the front window, nothing, you look out the back window, nothing, you look out the side window into the alley and there are six police cars,

Paulie in handcuffs, and Paulie's dead pit bull in a pile of blood. Later there will be a large tattoo of the dog's head on Paulie's left bicep, RIP Damien II. For a time there will be a shrine, prayer candles and flowers and a big rawhide bone, until the city puts a speed bump in the alley.

You were kind of getting used to the gunfire, but you hadn't yet seen it end with blood. It seemed to you like the gangbangers tended just to shoot and that whether or not they hit anything wasn't the point. The cops, in this incident anyway, hit their target.

When Little Paulie comes back the following summer, he looks even older, if that's possible, and there's a new girl in the house who looks different enough from Paulie and his possible sisters to guess she's a girlfriend, confirmed a few months later with the birth of Little Little Paulie. When Paulie the Third begins walking and talking, there is a spike in utterances of the name Paulie, which no doubt pleases the elder Little Paulie.

The summer Paulie comes back there's another new condo going up next to his house. The construction is on a loudness level comparable with Paulie and/or his transportation, and you can imagine that the loudness of construction versus the loudness of one guy, if that were your source of pride, would be a drag. It displeases Paulie, and it displeases you too, both because you could do without more Jennies and because it's also the summer you get burglarized and you suspect no one notices, at least partly because of the noise. But it pleases Jennie. *My property value has already doubled, practically! Someone down the hall sold their unit for twice what I paid!* You are sure the person she's talking to on the street is a casual acquaintance at best, if not a total stranger. You feel mildly uncomfortable thinking of an apartment as a unit. You tend not to think of your home as a unit. You are fairly sure that Paulie does not think about things like units and property value. You are fairly sure that Paulie was born in that house and will die in that house. Or near it. You are fairly sure you will leave when it's no longer cheap, which will be soon, and that more Jennies will follow. You don't know if this is good or bad.

You and Paulie acknowledge that you have seen one another on more than one occasion with nods, the kind where your head goes up and back, where you lead with your chin. Once, he held your door when you found a sweet chair in the alley. After the burglary, you ask a few neighbors, including Paulie, if they happened to see anything.

Paulie says no, but to let him know if you see anything again. *I know some people*, he says. You have a lot of thoughts about what this means. You secretly enjoy the idea that you know someone who knows some people who might do something very very bad on your behalf, even though you'd never ask. You are sure that Paulie does know some people. When something happens in the hood, Paulie is on the scene. You have seen him at the site of more than one car accident, looking on. You have even seen him on the local news, at the site of a car accident. You have seen him when the deli burned down and when the stabbing couple got taken away.

You try to avoid Jennie's side of the street, but she's seen you in the deli and you meet up in the cheese section at Whole Foods. You're carrying a handbasket containing a box of crackers and a wedge of Brie to bring to a potluck. Jennie has a cartful of everything and anything and when she sees you she greets you like an old friend and says *Can you believe these prices OMG I'm totally going to max out my card hey I'm having a sample sale you should totally come here's a flyer.* You enjoy the idea of discount designer clothes, but feel no more comfortable about having Jennie on your side than you do about Paulie.

Little Little Paulie, about three when you finally move, shows early signs of carrying on the Pagano family legacy. He drives his Playskool car with one hand on the top of the wheel and the other hanging out of the window. He looks worried, serious, almost exactly like his dad, except cute. But so far, you haven't heard him make a sound.

Some of My Intimates
Bob Hicok

Only after looking at the house going up
on the mountain across the valley, did I pick up
the fat Borges I've had for six years and read
a few paragraphs about Don Quixote, slipping
a pencil in the book when I was done and placing
the book on the table beside the window
through which I stared at the house.
There was an apple in my pocket with a flat spot
from when I dropped it on the floor.
It rolled under the table before I looked
at the house, and I got under the table
with the apple, the first time in my life
I'd been under a table with an apple.
I sat there a while, wondering what else
I haven't done, and then got up and looked
at the house and read some Borges. Don Quixote
has killed a man in the Borges. I screamed
when I read that, feeling this
is the honest response to murder when you have
a green apple in your pocket. The leaves
on the trees on the mountain
have turned gold and red and orange. I worry
the pencil will, over time, distort the book.
But now that I've put it there, I don't think
I should take it out, it seems
that I gave the moment a particular shape
by slipping the pencil between the pages,
and that to alter that shape now
would be a disavowal of my past. The light
on the Borges is gray. I imagine this

is the light that was touching Don Quixote
when he killed the man and that slipped
inside the wound of the man when he was killed.
It's light the sky keeps in a box
until it's winter. I hold the green apple
up to this light, it is my opposition, not to winter
but to what winter represents, to the house
going up on the mountain and the murder
in Borges that keeps happening every time
someone reads those pages. I suspect
there are feelings in the apple,
that I'll never know what it costs the apple
to go up against the gray light and the house
and the murder. A God would know this,
but what a God knows a man cannot know,
nor what a dog knows can a man know,
nor what a man knows can a man know.
They needed a road to put the house up, for days
a great felling of trees, the sound of it
a growling on the mountain. But in a few years,
no one will question that road, it will seem
as if the trees one day curtsied
and stepped out of the way. There was nothing
under the table except me and the apple
and my future and the apple's future.
It was an exciting moment of *esprit de corps*.

Auto Parts
Sarajane Woolf

1

The best auto parts store in, say, the galaxy, is in Guadalupe, California. A couple hundred miles up the coast from LA, it's where you want to be if you have the urge to buy a fan belt, new headlights, various oily fluids. Or you can just wander the aisles, like I did, and discover what you can't live without, maybe a sponge-squeegee combo like the one I use to thwart my windows' coastal grime. When you've finished shopping, you could offer to leave some little thing, testimony of another world—a bill in foreign currency; a campaign button for a battle now forgotten; a theater program culled from the floor of your backseat, particularly if the stars are known. A paw the size of a car engine, made of plaster now weathered—who left that?

2

North and west of Guadalupe, down a walkway raised above Oso Flaco Lake, past a sign warning of mountain lions and their preference for children, through dune scrub of native leathery-leaved plants, past the roped and sign-posted snowy plover nesting grounds, along the wild-waved ocean shore, across the inches-deep mouth of the Santa Maria River, I walked into the dunes. Although it was cool that April day, I trod barefoot, my soles massaged by sand. *Coreopsis gigantea*, a strange, cartoonish plant—thick trunk, three feet high or higher, rubbery leaves sprouting from the top in carrot-like proportions—dotted one hill. The blooming time gone, I saw a lone aster flower. The leaves, a brighter green than most drought-tolerant plants, had already begun to wilt and turn brown, as if paying the price for that color. Veering north, I shoe-surfed down small craters and crawled up the opposite sides, my legs moving just faster than the sand slid down. You can come to the edge of larger bowls, not knowing until you're there that below your next planned step the sand drops several feet. It feels wildly dangerous, though maybe it's not.

3

Sand. The plot of the second half of Cecil B. DeMille's 1923 version of *The Ten Commandments* turns on the misapplication of sand. Made long before Charlton Heston played Moses, the film opens with the biblical basics. It feels short, considering the commotion over the set—the biggest, grandest, costliest of the time—and frantic, relying for dramatic effect in this silent era on Big Eyes and Sweeping Arms. Featuring two twenty-something brothers, and their mother, who's at least eighty, the second half of the film jumps forward three millennia to show what happens in modern times when you break a bunch of commandments. The bad brother, a contractor building a church, skimps on the concrete mix, adding too much sand, and bribes the building inspector who notices. Later, when the bad brother's wife discovers his lunch-time tryst, she zooms up a construction lift to be consoled by the good brother, the job foreman. Bad concrete gives way under her feet, and she dangles from a convenient beam. Eventually the concrete church collapses, killing the mom; OSHA comes much later.

4

Halfway through Peter Brosnan's unfinished documentary on the sets and the making of *The Ten Commandments,* appears the title "Dana Walker, Saw the Jello." Dana says he was seven or eight or nine when he and a friend snuck onto the Paramount lot in the Guadalupe dunes and discovered DeMille's secret Red Sea. A round tank, maybe fifty feet across, held the Jell-O. Even though it was not very clean, the boys tasted it anyway. Who could resist that red? On film the gelatin is quivery and smooth in the role of state-of-the-art fake sea walls. After the Israelites traverse the sea floor, dripping edges of the parted fluid become buckets of water that bury the Pharaoh's troops. I watched *The Ten Commandments* after the documentary, fretting that the two Jell-O banks, if bumped, would slide into each other.

5

The Napa Auto Parts store in Guadalupe—"J. Perry Auto Supply, Inc." on a sales slip and "Napa Auto & Antiques" in a Chamber of Commerce brochure—is filled with glorious treasures, of sorts. As curator of his own collection, John Perry displays things meaningful to himself: the metal Phantoms car club symbol he forged in high school, the forty-five rpm record of Perry and the Biscaynes performing "Church Key" and "Moment of Truth," written by the Surfaris of "Wipeout" fame; things people might have discarded but instead gave to John: an ashtray from a defunct local bar, an old fire extinguisher; and things John acquired by his own volition: wood panel and glass walls from the old Post Office, "Parcel Post—Stamps—Registry" painted on frosted glass above the walk-up counter. These mingle with the new supplies. No lines stake out separate territories of merchandise for sale and antiques on display.

6

The dunes near Guadalupe have posed not just as Egyptian sand, but also as Algerian sand, in the 1926 film *Son of the Sheik*, Rudolph Valentino's last; Arizonan sand, in *The Water Hole*, a 1928 adaptation of Zane Grey's *Lost Pueblo*; Moroccan sand, in the 1930 film *Morocco* with Gary Cooper and Marlene Dietrich; and Sudanese sand, in "The Light that Failed," the 1939 film based on Rudyard Kipling's novel of the same title. All these places attributed to pieces of rock so small they shift with each breeze.

7

DeMille feared abandoning his sets when he finished filming *The Ten Commandments*. Another director could move in and spew out a low-budget movie faster than DeMille could release his. So, he buried them, leaving this clue in his autobiography: "If, a thousand years from now, archaeologists happen to dig beneath the sands of Guadalupe, I hope that they will not rush into print with the amazing news that Egyptian civilization, far from being confined to the valley of the Nile, extended all the way to the Pacific Coast of North America. The sphinxes they will find were buried there when we had finished with them and dismantled our huge set of the gates of Pharaoh's city." Hollywood studios have resisted Peter Brosnan's fundraising efforts to unearth, unsand the sets, but the Bank of America—founded by A. P. Giannini, who bailed out DeMille's film when Adolph Zukor balked at rising costs—paid for their archaeological mapping.

8
The Jell-O used for the parting Red Sea could have been raspberry, strawberry, or cherry. All these red Jell-Os were available at the time, in addition to orange, peach, and the brown and yellow flavors: chocolate and lemon. Originally introduced in 1904, chocolate was discontinued in 1927. Twenty-three years on the market—what happened? Did quivering umber suddenly seem portentous, causing us to squirm?

9
An early history of Santa Barbara County describes Guadalupe in 1874 as a "wide awake little village" with one hundred homes, six shops, five saloons, two hotels, two livery stables, one blacksmith shop, a Wells Fargo & Company express office, a post office (including the parts John owns), and a fruit store. I visited the town on a Friday, a fairly lively Friday, I thought, for a fairly remote town. Although it's on Highway 1, this isn't the stretch that coastal travelers might take for the scenery. The biggest excitement around town that day was the news that the mayor had racked up $5,600 in cell phone calls the previous year. "That guy made 160 calls a day!" John said, and the mayor wouldn't explain. Guadalupe—a town on the move.

10
Dune sand moved under my feet like dry sub-zero snow, but without the squeaky sound. Behind me, a brisk breeze rounded the edges and filled the valley of each footprint just as a blizzard of snow might. The bulk of the scenes for *Son of the Sheik* were filmed in Yuma, Arizona, where large fans whipped sand into a required storm. Fans were not needed for the shooting of *The Ten Commandments* in Guadalupe. In fact, the actors and actresses, protecting their eyes and faces between scenes with goggles and scarves, might have preferred less blowing sand.

11
A dramatic high point of Peter Brosnan's documentary centers on his desire to confirm the location of *The Ten Commandments* sets. He hoped they were buried in the dunes, but had no evidence other than local rumors and DeMille's book. Captured on film is Marilyn Stanley, employee of Holly Sugar, the company that owned the dunes land in 1923, a company deserving of a five-star award for record keeping. Ms.

Stanley was able to produce the original contract for Paramount's use of the land. It states that the said second party will dismantle all buildings erected on said property of first party and will remove therefrom all said material from said property and all of the refuse and rubbish within thirty days after the completion of said filming. Ms. Stanley next produced a copy of Holly Sugar's letter to Paramount confirming they had "complied with the terms of the agreement and left the land in proper condition." A geophysicist's investigations with ground penetrating radar proved Holly Sugar wrong.

12

I write as though I know that the gelatin for the parting of the Red Sea was Jell-O. But other brands of gelatin were available in 1923; Knox has been producing it since 1890, though that company didn't even consider flavored gelatin until 1936. Before commercial gelatin, derived from the animal hides and bones of selected abattoirs—a word that, to me, conjures boutique slaughterhouses—molded desserts and salads required cooks to mess around with soup bones or fish. These would be simmered, then cooled until a translucent jelly formed on the surface, ready to be reduced and clarified with egg whites. The gelatin could then be flavored, colored, textured by beating, and molded into shapes. Traditional Jell-O molds remind me of mythical cathedrals or mountaintops that loom above clouds and imply unattainable knowledge or unattainable fun. Especially in these shapes, the appeal of a transparent food was enormous, then as now.

13

A dirty, disembodied glove grabs the top of an oil can pyramid. The gold-plated wrenches John won at a Napa event are in the same display case as a soldering gun that you may want and an old photo of the local Druids' baseball team that you probably won't. I sense John's indiscriminate affection for everything in the shop: the staff carried by Rudolph Valentino in *Son of the Sheik*, a pig-skinning device, a Black & Decker drill, the original ticket shredder from the Royal Theatre down the street, a starter from a '41 Buick, small wood hieroglyphs that once projected from the movie set. The opposite of the temples in Egypt, where words on exteriors were painted or carved into walls, these hieroglyphs hint at a reverse Egyptian world, temples inflated until the carved forms pushed out.

14

Traditional concrete formulas from the turn of the century, and still used today, refer to cement, sand, and stone mixtures of 1:2:4, sand filling the space between stones, cement filling the space between grains of sand. Then water is added, inciting these particles to hydrate and harden. The bad brother in *The Ten Commandments* used twelve parts sand and apparently no stone, but is the good brother right when he says that made the concrete weak? After fifty thousand tests over six years on different concrete formulas, the Duff Abrams study of 1912 concluded, "The strength depends on only one factor—the ratio of water to cement." Aside from that, by the 1920s, ready-mixed concrete helped control the quality. The more-fascinating-than-you-might-think 1964 *Pictorial History of the Ready Mixed Concrete Industry* suggests it wouldn't have been as easy as DeMille implies to double the amount of sand: this was a new industry proving itself.

15

In the biblical half of *The Ten Commandments,* the set mimics the entrance to the temple of Luxor, with its colossal statues of Ramses II, the Pharaoh of the Old Testament's *Exodus*. It is not dissimilar to what might have stood behind the Colossi of Memnon, a pair of sixty-foot high statues built two centuries earlier. The real colossi now stand isolated in a fertile Egyptian field and seem as out of place as they would in a field of North Dakota wheat—or on a Guadalupe dune. The distant pyramid on the movie set seems merely to signify Egypt, anchoring the film there, rather than in ancient Guadalupe.

16

When my maternal grandmother died, a friend appeared at my mother's door, presenting a dish of fruit suspended in clear red Jell-O, because this is what their mothers would have done. I noted this courtesy, and, years later, when the young men three houses away were arrested one dawn for their lawless botanic enterprise, I thought of leaving a note at their door saying, "I'm sorry," with cookies, or Jell-O. They're nice men, helped me when my scooter blew a fuse and I didn't know what to do. Younger than I, they might have grown up on Jell-O flavors unknown in my youth. According to Kraft Foods literature, the '60s were a time of "flavor expansion and experimentation." Perhaps the course of these men's lives turned a corner when their mothers brought home wild cherry, wild strawberry, wild raspberry.

17
While I linger at Napa Auto Parts, two customers enter. One, a retiree, says he moved to Guadalupe from Seattle years ago, then tells me about his bypass surgery. When I say, "Take care of yourself," he tosses off the remark with a scowl, as if to say, "Why bother?" Another man, named Frank, wants to show something to John outside. "Want to watch the store?" John asks me, and barely noticing that I agree, leaves the shop. I'm in charge! I don't know if I should hope for customers or not. I continue browsing the shelves: a vacuum gage from the old ice plant, small cars of colored glass (Avon, I am later told), a menu from Leo's Drive-In (Bacon, fifty cents; Ham & Eggs, one dollar), a swan ornament for a '28 Chevy that once had a thermometer on the backside that could be read from the driver's seat.

18
Dozens of pieces of light green glass, each three-sixteenths of an inch thick, and not much longer or wider, lie scattered in the sand. All sides lightly etched, no longer transparent, but translucent, they catch and hold the sinking sun. I can't tell whether they've just been released from burial by the wind, or the opposite—that they will soon disappear. A display at the Dunes Center in Guadalupe recommends lying down on a dune to feel sand blowing over you and to hear its whisper. I am too busy collecting glass. My hand sweeping over the surface of the sand buries too many shards and picks up too much sand, but the pieces I leave will break down until indistinguishable from sand. The glass shards are waiting for me to pick them up and later build small pyramids on the glass surface of my desk. It's no worse than Mr. Brosnan saying the plaster sphinxes that lined the pathway to Ramses' temple await rescue from the dunes.

19
In the movie, the Pharaoh worships a scarab-headed god with appendages that recall antlers, though my insect field guide says they're antennae of leaf-like plates. This would be Khephri, the Egyptian god who played a major afterlife role during the New Kingdom. Scarabs

lay single eggs in balls of dung—why not?—and roll them around for forty days while each hosts a larva-nymph act that culminates in the emergence of a beautiful winged beetle. It's all symbolic—mud into life—and Khephri further represents spiritual potential. I think it's a mistake to worship potential. Just give me the winged creature. But I'd enjoy a closer look at Khephri exhumed, and after that, someone might like to have him. For years the Santa Maria Country Club had two of the movie's twenty-one five-ton sphinxes guarding their driveway entrance. Until succumbing to the elements, they were popular family photo props.

20
Alcohol was not allowed in Camp DeMille, where the film crew lived, but archaeological evidence indicates that high-alcohol cough syrup was not banned. Anyone who could drink that for fun would probably enjoy Jell-O shots. One party host, C. M. J. Baden of Anaheim, California, suggests combinations that have been "well received," though he thinks they are rather timid—raspberry schnapps with raspberry Jell-O, Grand Marnier with orange Jell-O. He prefers the heartier Irish whiskey sour Jell-O: 1 small lemon Jell-O, 1 small lime Jell-O, ½ cup Irish whiskey, 2 cups boiling water and 1½ cup cold water; and his World Famous Margarita Jell-O: 1 large lime Jell-O, ½ cup tequila, ¼ cup Triple Sec, 2 cups boiling water and 1¼ cup cold water. Mr. Baden does not recommend substituting all water with alcohol.

21
When John returns, he shows me an old turning light that, attached to the side of a truck, was operable by the driver flipping it down to indicate a turn and flipping it up when heading straight. John has mounted this signal to some shelves, next to new tail-light lens caps. By now we are friends, and I compliment him on the nice juxtaposition of the old and new lights. And while examining a photo of a handsome young man and his '53 Buick Skylark, John admits it was him, and I say, with approval, "Look at you!"

22
The historical location for the biblical parting of the sea, and whether in fact it was the Red Sea, is not known. The words used in the Bible,

yam suph, translate as "sea of reeds" and may mean the swampier area to the north. Narrower and shallower, fifteen or twenty miles wide, this location makes more sense than the one-hundred-and-fifty-mile wide Red Sea. Maybe DeMille knew this. The first encounter with the sea in the movie shows, well, not exactly a sea of reeds, but it's not one hundred and fifty miles wide either. Land in the background looks a lot like San Luis Obispo Bay, not much more than seventeen miles from Guadalupe. And the waves in the foreground look a lot like the Pacific Ocean, but that's neither here nor there. When DeMille watched his Israelites practice walking a straight path between lines of poles that represented edges of the future Jell-O banks, he was disturbed by the cleanliness of the sand they trudged—a groomed beach, not a drained sea. Think of the hair and scum left in the bottom of your drained tub. Just before the final filming at the zenith of the sun (to avoid shadows cast from the poles), he clamored into the ocean and grabbed armfuls of kelp to line the Israelites' path.

23

Although *The Ten Commandments* was filmed nearly eighty years ago, Peter Brosnan found a few local residents who remembered the event. One segment in his documentary features Ernie Righetti, who, when asked if the filming was something he's never forgotten, replies informatively, "That's right." Another gentleman recalls renting unbroken horses to the film crew that spilled boys all over the road, adding that while he enjoyed the spectacle at the time, when you get older you don't do those tricks anymore. Actor Pat Moore, who played the Pharaoh's son, says it wasn't that hard to play dead when he was carried to the Pharaoh: "You just let your arms go out." Excellently playing dead in part two of the film is Edythe Chapman. After she's killed by her son's collapsing church, her arms go out in much the same manner as Pat Moore's when the good son carries her to his brother. Some of the old timers interviewed are now dead, and while Mr. Brosnan may not be able to rescue the sets, his great legacy may be the capture of these men's words.

24

Howard Hansen, bless his soul, maintains a web site devoted to a home version of Creating the Red Sea in Jell-O. Intending to liven up Passover with some wholesome fun, he explains, "This is a family event, so we tend to downplay the whole killing thing." He's referring to the first-born-son killing thing, not the Red-Sea-collapsing-on-the-Pharaoh's-troops killing thing. He starts with a brilliant yellow Nubian-Arabian Jell-O desert in a rectangular baking pan. An aluminum foil dam—weighted down with coffee mugs and an All-Clad four-quart pan—blocks out space for the sea. After the yellow Jell-O solidifies, he carefully removes the foil; it sticks to the Jell-O, he warns. I thank Howard for coining the term "Jell-O shards," the stuck bits and the pieces that slip under the foil and need to be removed. "Create terrain," he suggests as a use for the shards, and this geographical fix looks quite realistic in his photo. Next, he pours un-gelled red Jell-O into the blank space, and when set, this is the Red Sea. It's easy to imagine what happens next: a slash down the middle of the Jell-O, children's fingers pulling back the edges of the sea, other fingers safely traversing the bottom of the pan, more fingers running as flaps of Jell-O sea are released.

25

Real and pretend history blend when the buried Ten Commandments sets are billed as an archaeological find. Stirring this hash is the plea for funds to uncover these sets, whether to acknowledge them as a work of art or to enact the perfect finale for Peter Brosnan's documentary film. Time equals deterioration, the story now reads, though I would think dry sand not the worst embalmer. The Dunes Center in Guadalupe honors the sets, devoting as much, if not more, space to their mystery than to the endangered snowy plovers that nest in the oceanside margins of the dunes. Save the plaster temple, save the plovers, bring back chocolate Jell-O, and don't throw anything away—give it to John. In California landfills, new garbage is covered almost immediately and always by that night. Landfills in other states are more fun to visit. People rummage around, take things home—sometimes more than they leave—and ponder big questions: what should be saved, what should be buried, what should remain underground? A 1930 Chevy Repair Manual, vintage fuzzy dice, sphinxes made in Hollywood, a shattered windshield glistening where a buggy drew lines in sand, snowy plovers huddled on one side, the rest of us hot-rodding on the other.

A Near Life Experience
RON SAVAGE

During her fifty-two years, Erma Rapoport imagined having an active social life, particularly when it came to her neighbor of at least twenty of those fifty-two years, the wonderful Mr. Whoever. Once she secretly observed him tending his garden through her mail-order 20 x 30 mm Explorer binoculars—this being in the fall of '81 or '82—and his eyes caught her attention. He had the kindest, dearest eyes she had ever seen, a grayish-blue, unusual eyes that could probably look deep inside a person and touch the heart. Oh, my, she thought, and cooled her flushed cheeks with quick little waves of her hand.

Then yesterday Mr. Whoever died, a massive coronary. The shock of his abrupt departure took Erma's breath away. She saw the James City County EMS truck in front of his house, its blue-and-red lights flashing. Ten or fifteen minutes later, a fat balding man and a rough-looking blonde woman, both wearing navy blue jackets, wheeled out a gurney with a plastic body bag strapped to it, presumably Mr. Whoever. The following day, she read his obituary and, after more than two decades, learned his name—Alvin Lipka. What's Lipka . . . Polish? She thought she knew a couple of Lipkas, maybe.

He was, or had been, a fifty-eight-year-old bachelor who was survived by no one, the poor thing.

If Erma had possessed the nerve to leave her house, she would've called one of those yellow cabs and gone to his funeral, but she hadn't been outside since childhood, when Mama had swept her to this physician and that. At the age of eleven—after seven exploratory surgeries and numerous poisonous bouts with her crazy mother's homemade medicines—Erma had acquired a diagnosis that satisfied everyone except Mama, though it *did* stop the madness. Munchausen Syndrome by proxy, the doctor called it, named after Baron von Munchausen, the eighteenth century traveler, adventurer, and liar. Erma's daddy, a withdrawn but generous man who more than likely felt some guilt for not curbing his wife's insatiable desire for medical attention, decided to leave his daughter a trust fund that contained enough money to avoid every human being on the planet for the rest of her life.

Instead of going to her neighbor's funeral, Erma lit a candle and placed it on the dining room windowsill, facing the glassed-in sunporch side of Mr. Lipka's house, may he rest in peace, briefly wondering if the dear man with the beautiful grayish-blue eyes would have approved.

On the second day after his death, while changing a used candle for a fresh one, she glanced out the window and saw a small hairy person sitting on Alvin Lipka's roof.

Then the small hairy person wrapped a tail about its shoulders like a comforting arm.

Erma immediately dug around in the hall closet for her mail order 20 x 30 mm Explorer binoculars, hoping to get a better view. And there it was, huddled by the chimney and trembling, a small gray monkey wearing a red fez tied beneath the chin and a matching red vest. Panning the binoculars down to the window of the glassed-in sunporch, she stared into the room and saw the top of a large brass cage . . . and the door was open. Case solved, Erma thought. Now she'd make a call to the SPCA, and that would be that. But what if they asked her name? Erma wasn't the type who talked to others. She certainly didn't want people traipsing around her clean house, leaving dirt on Mama's Oriental carpets, requiring soft drinks and snacks. Give an individual an inch and you've got yourself a friend attached at the hip. Still, you *ought* to call, she thought. You can't just let a helpless creature starve to death, or worse . . . become the supper of who-knows-what.

Erma was about to have another look at the monkey, but she heard a soft tapping sound at the front door. This got her anxious enough to drop the binoculars. She muttered the word "fudge" under her breath, and walked to the door, gazing into the peep hole. Erma was about halfway done scanning the wood stoop when the monkey's face enveloped her entire line of vision. Erma screamed. Then the monkey screamed. That's when she called the SPCA, said what she had to say, and clicked down the receiver. She felt her heart beating hard inside her chest. What a hideous day, what a completely, totally, hideous day. Erma leaned toward the front door, maybe a bit more warily than needed, though better safe than sorry, and she gazed again into the peep hole. The monkey laid sprawled on its back, the red fez cocked over a closed eye, its hairy hand clutching its chest as though preparing for cardiac arrest.

Oh, God, Mama was right, everything she touched turned to poop. But she *had* called the SPCA Shouldn't that count for something—sensitivity, intelligence, something? Then another thought occurred: What would happen if the monkey died on her front porch? Think of the embarrassing questions, think of all those SPCA people walking on her clean Oriental rugs, think of all the sodas and snacks. There'd be an inquiry, obviously, an unrelenting court battle. Her attorney would have to convince a jury of animal lovers how the deceased had a previously diagnosed heart condition. Veterinarians from opposing camps would testify. The news media would park outside her home, TV cameras poised to go off at the slightest hint of her presence.

Erma looked through the peephole for a third time. The porch was empty, the monkey gone. Thank you, thank you. Though . . . reflecting on it, what exactly did they do to a person who made felonious calls to the SPCA? Any individual who'd phone regarding a monkey ought to have the monkey available, or at least be able to show where such a monkey might spend its day. Isn't there some sort of law?

The sound of breaking glass followed by a now familiar screech came from the dining room. The monkey had managed to tear a hole in the window screen and climb into the house, knocking down Mr. Lipka's Memorial Candle. This had caused one of the Oriental rugs to catch fire. The monkey was currently being obsessive, turning around and around on the dining room table, its hideous toenails digging into the polished mahogany. Erma screamed. Then the monkey screamed. As Erma stomped out the fire with her blue terrycloth slippers, the monkey leaped onto the glass chandelier and swayed back and forth like, well, a monkey. Erma screamed again. Her unwanted guest darted into the living room, leaving a wake of smelly dark pellets. Erma was about to do another shriek when the doorbell rang. On her way to the living room, she paused at the peephole just long enough to see a white Humane Society van parked at the curb and a man with no chin peering back at her. He was probably trying to figure who called, she thought. Erma muttered the S-word under her breath and continued pursuing the hairy little beast who wouldn't stop relieving itself on her lovely rugs.

She found the monkey hiding under the Victorian sofa, a perfectly lovely piece, all forest-green velvet, not that the thing under the sofa cared. It hung upside down, its gray tail wrapped about a narrow wooden slat, the red fez now cupping its right ear.

"What a mess you are," Erma said.

She'd gotten down on her knees, head tilted to see the creature, but its face was turned away, obscured in the shadows. Before she could utter a second sentence, the monkey bounded past her, scampering across the oak-wood foyer. When Erma finally got to the Mr. Lipka Memorial Candle Window, she saw the man with no chin scooping the monkey into a net. Automatically, she stepped back, not wanting to be seen by . . . that wasn't clear, maybe she didn't want to be seen by the man, maybe she didn't want to be seen by the monkey.

As her days without Mr. Lipka continued, Erma adjusted. The burned spot on her mother's dining room rug could not be repaired, though the other Oriental rugs had been scrubbed and deodorized, the little black pellets carted off in plastic baggies. But an odd thing happened when she was scrubbing the rug in the living room. Erma had smiled, the thought of poop covering Mama's carpet seemed—what could a person do?—amusing. Then she laughed out loud and immediately chided herself for having such a crude sense of humor. What was so funny about ruining someone's perfectly lovely Oriental carpet; an antique, for God's sake? Especially Mama's carpet: what sort of wicked child laughed at that?

About the time everything was clean and in its proper place, a pale blue flyer came in the mail announcing a yard sale at Mr. Lipka's house. "All items MUST go," it said. "All $$$ REASONABLE $$$ offers accepted." Beneath this was the name Markus Teller, Esq., Attorney. A sadness swept over Erma, and she wasn't sure why, except the pale blue flyer had left her with the feeling of finality.

That night she went to bed and dreamed of the monkey in the red fez and red vest. The annoying hairy thing had done an enormous poop on her mother's mahogany dining room table. It leaped up and down in the poop with both hands and feet like a deliriously happy child playing in a mudhole. Then the monkey began running up the walls, springing a speedy two-step onto the ceiling, its fall ending in a quick backflip and perfect landing. Over and over it did this, occasionally dabbing its hands and feet in the poop the way an artist freshens his brush. The impulsive creature also found Mama's white curtains and wrapped its hairy poop-matted body in the folds of the material. It rolled itself around on the dining room rug, too, making joyful *che-che-che* sounds. By the time Mr. Lipka's monkey was finished, mama's cheery dining room had taken on a morose brown tint and smelled like a clogged toilet. Erma laughed until the tears wet her cheeks. Funny as a rubber crutch, that's what her once-upon-a-time friend Jenny Rizzo used to say in third grade. Funny as a rubber crutch, girl.

She gave fifty dollars to one of the neighborhood boys to buy the monkey's brass cage at Mr. Lipka's yard sale. She even let the boy inside her house so he could set it up in the living room by the bay window. A day later Erma was gazing at the stupid cage with its little swings and ropes. She didn't have a clue as to why she'd thrown fifty dollars down the crapper for a pile of useless metal. Erma had lived in this house her entire life and the cage was the first item she had bought to put inside the place, her very own piece. Though mother died in '96 from pancreatic cancer—the irony of *that* had not gone unnoticed—and her father had suffered a long respiratory illness culminating in his death two years ago, it'd always been *their* house.

Erma liked coming downstairs in the morning and seeing the brass cage beside the bay window in the living room. She particularly liked how the sun reflected off the metal, flecking the white walls with bits of dazzling light. It reminded her of the disco movie *Saturday Night Fever*. Erma ordered polish to keep the brass new and bright. She told the grocer to send her more fruits, too: some watermelon and papaya, some bananas and cantaloupe, that sort of thing.

After Erma finished breakfast, she would chop up the fruits into bite-sized pieces and put them in the tiny brass food bowl hooked to the cage. Along with that, she filled the brass water bowl with Evian. Then Erma would sit in the salmon-colored high back, her mother's favorite chair, and pretend the monkey was there eating the fruits. She decided to call him Alvin, hoping Mr. Lipka would be pleased. Erma imagined going over to the cage, Alvin tipping his red fez and reaching out. He would grasp her finger, climb gently up her arm and perch on her shoulder, his soft tail curling about her neck. He'd stare up at her with those eyes, the kindest, dearest eyes she'd ever seen, grayish-blue, unusual eyes that could probably look deep inside a person. She would tell him about the two floors above them and what was there, the places where Mother kept all her personal things that you were never allowed to touch.

three maps
RICK MOODY

Figure 1. Melancholy in the Greater Dallas–Fort Worth Area

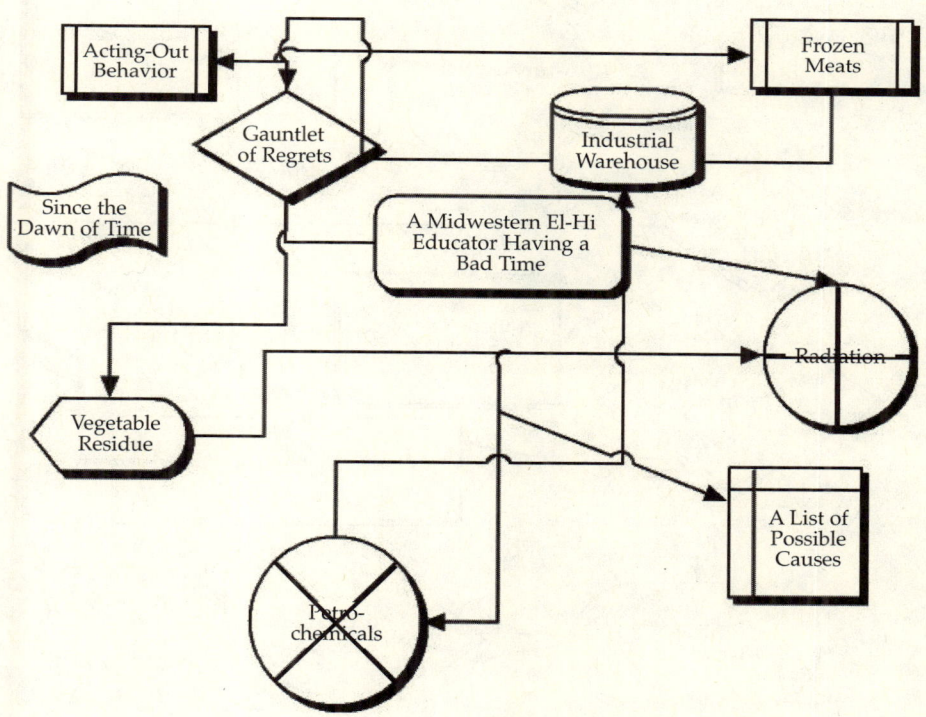

Figure 3. How to Drive Off Your Last Friend

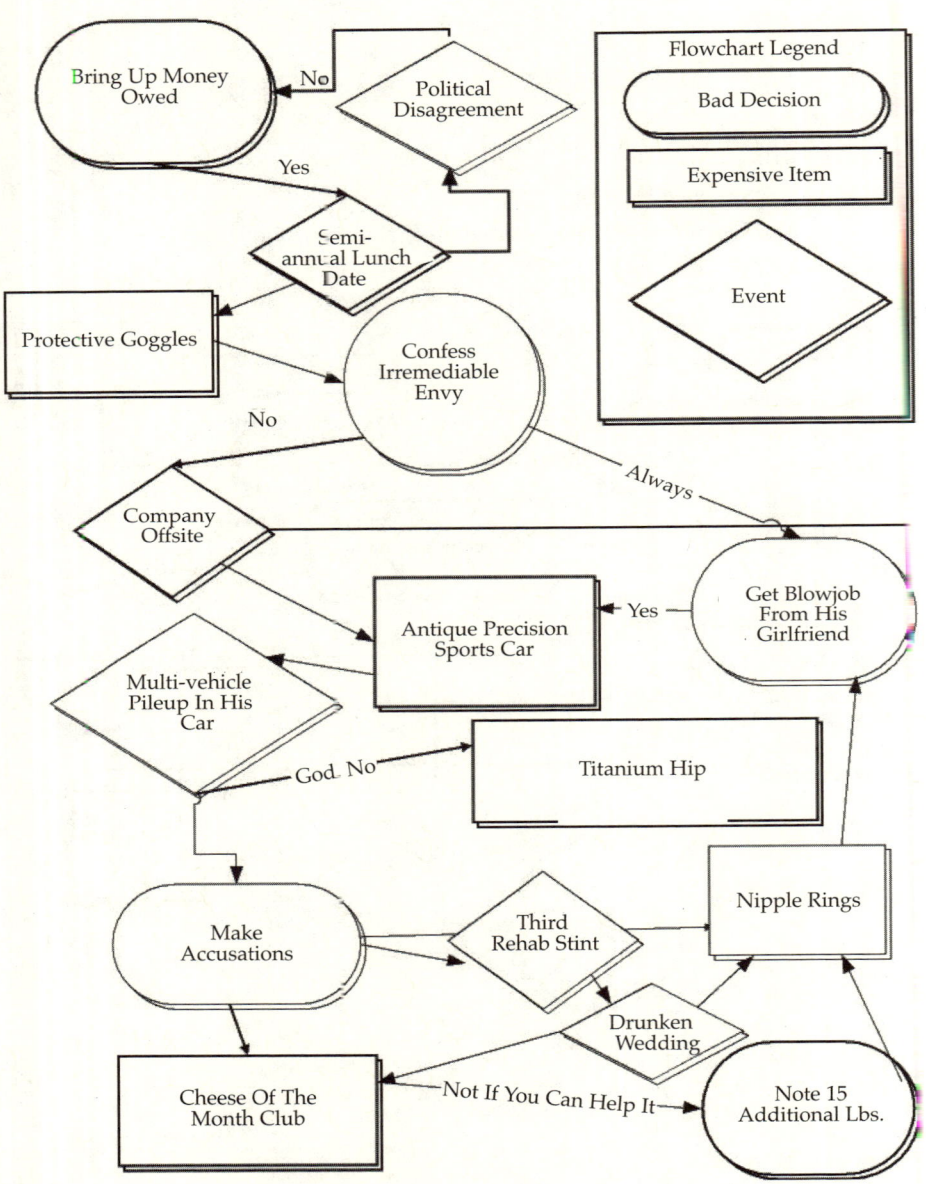

Figure 5. Several Jelly Doughnuts Mistakenly Believe They Are Particle Collider

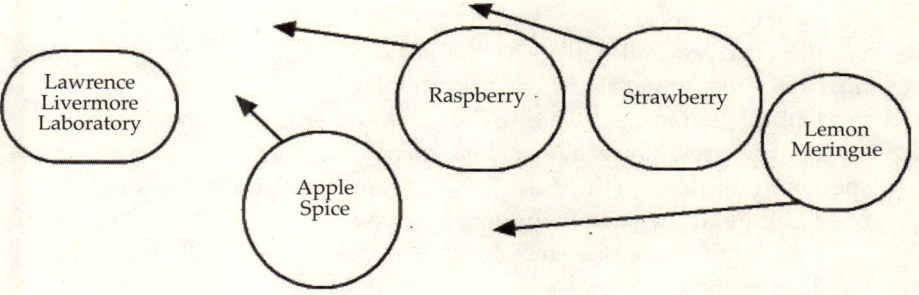

(Particle Collider Not To Scale)

By Canoe Into My Father's War
Terry Marshall

Chief Willie powers our dugout down the Rendova coast as if time matters in the Solomon Islands. The wake from his 25-horse Tohatsu engine ruffles a glassy sea. Its shrieking wail assaults the Sabbath morning.

Without warning, Chief cuts starboard, then slows. The man-made breeze dies and sweat drips from beneath my hat, drenches my shirt. It's early December.

Bare-chested and hatless, Willie points landward. "*Iu lukim desfala riva?* Do you see that river?" he asks in Pijin.

Unbroken forest stretches to the sea, hiding the coastline. No markers identify a river: no roads, no houses, no bridges, no silt-laden plume spewing into this pristine bay. I finally locate a crack in the jungle. A river emerges from beneath the dense canopy. "*Ies, mi lukim.* Yes, I see it."

"My land ends at the river."

"Your land?"

"Ughele's land. Our village land," he says.

We've been cruising at breakneck speed since we left Ughele thirty minutes ago. How far does his land run on the other side of Ughele village?

His answer translated from the Pijin: "Long way, little bit."

Forty-five minutes later, we zoom through a reef passage into the bay facing isolated Lokuru village. Willie cuts the engine, and our other passenger—Radio—leaps into waist-deep water and drags the canoe onto the beach. Radio's not a nickname. His father served as lookout to a GI radio operator in World War II. It's the family's badge of honor. He's my age, fifty.

Chief and I step dry-footed onto coral sand so dazzling it seems to singe the extra-heavy tint from my prescription sunglasses.

Lokuru has no resident minister, so Willie, chief of Ughele village, doubles as aide to Pastor, Rendova's circuit-riding preacher. I'm

Willie's houseguest, back in the Solomons to train a group of new Peace Corps volunteers. This 1991–1992 stay is my second in the Solomons, an 870-mile-long chain of islands northeast of Australia. My wife and I lived here from 1977 to 1980 when we directed the Peace Corps in this part of the South Pacific. I'm alone this trip. My wife's back in Colorado with our two kids, the younger of whom was born in the Solomons.

We scrub off the salt spray in the village creek. In mid-morning heat, this tepid water seems as cool as a Rocky Mountain stream. Willie leaves to prepare for the service. I linger.

Willie returns in Sabbath uniform: dark pants, long-sleeved white shirt, and tie. He escorts me into the dirt-floored church, and as sweat soaks my walking shorts, Chief Willie delivers his sermon as coolly as if it were an October day in Colorado. In Pijin, spiced with passages in Lokuru, he hammers together relevant point, concise anecdote, Biblical quote, and plank by plank builds his irrefutable message that God's love holds salvation for every Solomon Islander, and—with a nod toward me—for our visiting white man.

Saturday, the Sabbath in a Seventh-Day Adventist village, isn't for the faint of heart. We worship from ten until one. Hand-hewn planks serve as backless pews. They offer no comfort.

All Lokuru gathers to feed us before we head back to Ughele. With the village men, we stand elbow to elbow at a fifty-foot-long plank table. We pile "room temperature" charred fish and yams, gummy taro pudding, and warm pineapple onto banana leaves, then eat with sticky fingers. Beyond an invisible cordon, women and children silently stare. They'll eat what we leave behind.

En route home, Willie edges into thick mangroves hiding a bank of pitted limestone. He points and says, "See the markings on the rock. In the war, Japanese hid here. We killed them."

World War II sites dot the Rendova coast. Willie shouts a history of each as we pass. Near Ughele, he cuts the engine and points out a cave. "The Japanese hid here also, inside. I went first. I'm chief," he says, drifting into another Pijin story, a time-honed recital performed by lapping one theme over another, rephrasing each coda in a new key, glissading forward, doubling back until a clear aria emerges somehow from a vague medley. Here are the translated highlights, a tenth of the original: Barefoot and in loincloth, Willie creeps forward, Marine Raider knife in hand. He bends no leaf, makes no sound. A sentry steps out. Willie executes him. He motions his men forward. Like shadows they skulk from the jungle. Two carry captured Arisaka 7.7 mm rifles, the others spears and clubs. They charge the two dozen Japanese holed up here. Willie's men take no prisoners and gain an arsenal of modern weapons.

Willie recounts this 1943 event as if he were rehashing this morning's sermon in Lokuru.

Wait a sec. Chief Willie's fity-two, only two years my elder. He'd have been a toddler during the war. His stories memorialize his people's history, not his personal experience.

Back in Ughele, on Willie's veranda fronting the bay, the nightly feast far surpasses lunch in Lokuru. Radio joins us, grabs a barbecued coral trout. "At dawn, tide, moon, and weather will converge. Fish will run beyond the point," he says. Willie nods. We'll take his canoe.

Willie's son-in-law Raouli heaps his plate with fish and taro. "In America, do black men teach school?" he asks. He's a primary teacher, home for Christmas break with his wife, Chief's eldest daughter. "Of course," I say, and for an hour we talk race, politics, and history. Pastor joins us. Village men I've not yet met slip into vacant spaces on the bench lining the veranda, blend instantly into the ongoing stories. One regales us with a tale of a youthful pig-stealing sortie, or was it a raid on a Japanese rice cache? Time seems suspended in these stories, irrelevant.

Willie says a Japanese tuna boat will dock tomorrow or the next day at Ughele wharf. Welcoming plans emerge over mounds of four-inch-long pan-fried fish. Somehow, we drift back to 1943. Willie leads us as we rescue a downed American pilot. We paddle all night through enemy-infested seas and sigh with relief as torrential rain gives us cover. We ambush Japanese patrols. We signal up and down the coast, warning of bomber waves zeroing in on Guadalcanal—all the while nibbling from bowls and platters on the picnic bench that serves as Willie's dining table. No alcohol loosens our tongues or dulls our minds. Seventh-Day Adventists don't drink.

Night wears on. I slip away to my bedroom, adjacent to the veranda. The storytellers dwindle, until, finally, voices cease. I lie awake inside a tent of white mosquito netting, my mind buzzing with today's events. Willie's stories bring World War II to life. Yet his unmasked pride in killing repudiates his pious sermon in Lokuru. No wonder he led "Onward Christian Soldiers" with gusto. He's a soldier reveling in his exploits. No, wait—he's reveling in his father's exploits.

I flip on my flashlight, prop it against my camp pillow so I can scribble today's notes into my journal. No one wears a watch in Ughele. Mine reads 11:42 p.m. Like time, dates have no meaning here. My journal tells me otherwise: today is December 7, 1991. Fifty years ago to the day, Japan bombed Pearl Harbor and yanked America into World War II. Today, in Ughele, Rendova, Solomon Islands, World War II lives on, as surely as if it were fought last week.

Several days pass. Late in the afternoon, I close the four-room primary school, padlock the one lockable room. I'm beat. A rancorous staff meeting unmasked a festering feud among our Pijin teachers, Solomon Islanders all. For two hours, we yammered over one teacher's incessant complaints: no one works as hard as she; she lacks this, and that. The barrage of Pijin has given me a headache. I head for the village bathing pond to wash away the stains of verbal battle.

For the quarter mile from school to Chief Willie's house, Ughele's main street is two parallel dirt trails through foot-trod field grass, as if wagon trains once passed through. Yet, there are no cars, no trucks, not even a bicycle or wheelbarrow, no beasts of burden in Ughele.

The only sound is my sandals scuffing through field grass. No radios. No TVs. No phones ringing. When I stop, silence. In the distance, a child laughs, a woman's muted voice responds. The sounds fade. Wild shrieks shatter the quiet. A band of blazing colors screeches through the treetops: parrots. They alight, fall silent. I walk on. No dogs nip at my heels or bark when I pass.

An outboard engine echoes across the bay. I locate it, a distant shadow against the reflected sun. Chief Willie could tell me who the canoe belongs to and who's driving. He knows each engine by its whine, each driver by the canoe's movements.

The grass dies out beyond Willie's, and the path widens. The concrete wharf is fifty feet to the left. Here Ughele congregates on Monday mornings around a horseshoe of wooden stalls to sell produce to passengers on the inter-island ship, *Iuminao*, when it pauses en route to Gizo from Guadalcanal. Now the stalls are deserted. Late tonight the arena will buzz with milling teenagers when, sans food, drink, or souped-up cars, these stalls serve as Ughele's Sonic drive-in.

A half-mile from Willie's house, the path narrows to footprint width. I tightrope across the makeshift bridge, a pair of palm logs, over a small creek that marks the village's eastern boundary and arrive at the stream with its sauna-sized natural pool where most village men and children bathe. Usually it's clear as a Rocky Mountain spring. This evening I'm late, the water murky.

Like most Solomon Islands communities, Ughele violates the American image of a proper village. Even with one thousand residents—huge by Solomon Islands standards—Ughele has no business district, no plaza anchored by church and government office, no cantina. No malls, cafés, social clubs or sporting events provide diversion. No movies offer escape. I can't wander down to the post office or buy a Coke at the general store. Ughele has neither. Ughele is a mile of thatched huts winding along the bay in two zig-zag rows.

Chief houses me in relative luxury. I sleep on a foam pad atop a raised wooden platform. Willie's compound has a water-seal pit toilet, built for our arrival, but I'm the only one using it. Villagers use designated areas in the open near the beach. Chief has a diesel-powered generator, and our house alone has electricity—a couple of hanging lightbulbs, no refrigeration. Our house has tightly thatched roof and walls, hard-packed dirt floor, cut-outs for windows and doors.

Chief's veranda is the center of adult Ughele social life. An ever-shifting assembly of men provides fellowship. Tonight I last until 11:30 before the repetition of familiar stories and small talk wears me down. I listen from my bunk. Finally, words blur, and I drift off.

2:12 a.m., awake again. The blessed light zeros in like an interrogation lamp. Willie, wearing only frayed walking shorts, no shirt, sleeps without pillow, padding, or mosquito net on the hardwood bench that borders the veranda and sea wall. I wrap on my *lavalava*, slip into the main room, unplug the lights. Night engulfs us. The generator drones on. Sometime in the night someone turns it off, or it runs out of petrol. Willie's gone at 4:33 when I awake again.

Christmas morning, 1991: no rats yet, but for the sixty-seventh night running some unknown force jars me awake long before dawn. This morning, 2:57 a.m.

The tropics should mean carefree sleep. Palm fronds rustle outside my room. Rendova Bay laps gently twenty feet away. A white net shields me from the malaria-laden mosquitos, but equally as important, from rats. They dash along the hand-hewn rafters as if beams were catwalks to battle stations. They bash about like drunken sailors, squealing, roughhousing, leaping. I have yet to sleep more than two hours at a stretch since I arrived in the Solomons nine weeks ago.

Wide awake in the dark, I am overtaken by eerie images. A snap, a muffled voice: a commando skulks outside, any moment to burst into the room, stiletto flashing. A squeak: Rat? Bat? A signal to attack? The enemy parrots jungle sounds, you know.

My mission to Rendova is for the Peace Corps, but war dominates my thoughts. Are these visions Chief Willie's stories coming back to haunt me? My own imagination gone berserk?

In July 1943, across the channel beyond Willie's veranda, raw GIs on New Georgia faced a similar night huddled in foxholes, not beds. The jungle spooked them: shadows, faint sounds, nothing at all. A panicky GI fired a shot. Terrified men popped from their foxholes to pepper the black jungle. In one week, the US Army evacuated 360 jittery soldiers to Guadalcanal. That incident spurred research that identified combat neurosis—war nerves. The men snapped under strain and exhaustion and intimidating jungle. Most of those soldiers were younger than the thirty-two American Peace Corps trainees with me in Ughele.

We Peace Corps have been in Ughele only twenty-four days, but complaints mount. Cold fish and yams no longer make a quaint breakfast. Drought continues and sections of the village have no water; the volunteers and their host families must haul it from the stream for cooking. The water-seal pit toilets promised by Chief Willie haven't been built. They're tired of trekking off to a feces-strewn beach to relieve themselves or to change a tampon. Classes drag on. The first-blush judgment that Pijin is mere baby-talk English has been rudely shot down as we teach subtle forms needed to express doubt or anticipated action. Trainees and staff form cliques. Rumors flourish as if sprouted from magic beans. Sore throats, sunburn, and diarrhea sap energy, and coral scrapes set nerves on edge. Three trainees contract malaria. Irritations fester. Christmas dawns in tropical heat, without mall Santas or decorated trees. Yet I find myself feeling more sympathy for the fears of those frightened soldiers on New Georgia than for the complaints of my own charges.

This week's mail has brought an unexpected package from a World War II veteran, Col. George Tuck. He'd called me after reading my article about Solomon Islands war hero Jacob Vouza in *Retired Officer Magazine*, and he and I had discussed writing a book together about the war on Guadalcanal when I left for this assignment in the Solomons.

Tuck arrived in the Solomons with a glider squadron in mid-1943. By then, Guadalcanal was a staging base, not the battlefront, and Tuck had free time aplenty. A farmer from Oklahoma, he sent for seeds from an uncle. He gardened. He explored the island. He met Solomon Islanders.

Tuck's package includes a dozen photos from 1943: bomb-shredded palms barren as scarred telephone poles; shirtless GIs with two Solomon Islanders, all stiff and unsmiling, as if facing a Matthew Brady field camera; a downed Japanese bomber, GIs posed at nose and tail as if each personally had shot it from the sky. The prize photo is young Tuck, a swaggering pilot with shoulder pistol and pith helmet, beside a muscular forty-five-year-old Jacob Vouza, M-1 at parade rest.

Vouza was a bona fide war hero before Tuck met him. The Japanese captured Vouza, an allied scout, early in the war. When he refused to talk, they tied him to a tree, bayoneted him, slit his throat, and left him to die. Vouza chewed through the rope, then crawled and stumbled miles through jungle and raging battle to report enemy positions to his company commander.

Tuck and Vouza became friends. A marksman with a rifle, Vouza one day pointed to Tuck's .45 and asked to fire it. "After a few clips he was a good shot. A few more, and he was an expert," Tuck recalls. Fascinated by airplanes, Vouza asked Tuck to take him flying.

"Can't," Tuck said. "Against regulations."

Vouza insisted. Tuck flew him on his first air view of Guadalcanal, filing his flight plan as a solo training jaunt. Next day, Vouza returned: "Take me again. I will jump out."

"He was fearless, but I couldn't go that far," Tuck said.

"Another afternoon, a buddy and I strolled off to a creek to bathe. From nowhere, a shot rang out. We hightailed it out. Later, we told Vouza about it. He took off and returned a couple of days later with a bloody gunny sack. 'Jap fella no shootum at fly boys no more ever,' Vouza told us. We didn't have the stomach to look inside the sack."

I knew Jacob Vouza as an old man in the late 1970s, white haired, slow of foot, hard of hearing. He would come to the Peace Corps office in Honiara, the capital city, when he needed a ride home. His village, California, was twenty miles by washboard road and jeep trail up the Guadalcanal coast. He believed America remained his staunchest ally. I often drove him home.

Tuck's photos remind me of one I found in the National Archives in Washington, DC: a gang of GIs and nurses piled on a Willys Jeep at a Guadalcanal river, hamming it up like college kids on spring break. I compare it to my own snapshots of Peace Corps volunteers on weekend outings. Trade the Willys for a Suzuki. Substitute shorts and T-shirts for khaki dungarees. Let crew cuts sprout into shaggy mops. That 1943 shot could easily be 1979 or 1992. I suspect the ceaseless carping of Peace Corps volunteers sounds much like the endless griping of GIs.

I'm compelled by Tuck's photos and Chief Willie's war stories to organize an excursion to Lumberia Island, ninety minutes west of Ughele, in Chief's enormous motorized dugout. In 1943, Lumberia had been an American PT base. Lt. John F. Kennedy was stationed there.

We pack a picnic lunch before we go. Someone scrounges up a hand of bananas and a fresh pineapple. Two of us go shopping. The only woman in the village who bakes bread has sold her day's supply, so we search out a store to see what we can get. No signs identify Ughele's four stores—no hand-scrawled *Joe's Tienda*, no advertisements for Coca-Cola, no Open/Closed signs. Each is merely a window-front on its owner's thatch hut. I locate a store. It sells only a score of basic items: tinned tuna, matches, Navy biscuits, fishing line, and three aluminum pots. We settle for a bundle of concrete-hard Navy biscuits and several tins of Solomon Blue tuna, the inexpensive grade of choice among Peace Corps volunteers, a grade sold as cat food in the US.

Lumberia Island is uninhabited, but a hand-scrawled sign confirms that President Kennedy lived here. Lumberia's what World War II should be in the 1990s: shards and scraps. I photograph a rusted machine gun planted like a lawn ornament beside the sign, and tromp among slivers of cement pilings. The island has a war museum: a windowless one-room leaf hut. It's padlocked. Little else attests to that fifty-year-old war—a length of rusted pipe, man-made depressions here and there. No docks. No decrepit buildings. We conjure up images of JFK and his crew tying PT-109 to a now-phantom dock. Not far from here, in August 1943, Biuku Gasa and Aaron Kumana paddled Lt. Kennedy and his PT-109 crew to safety. Today's Lumberia presents none of Hollywood's drama. Nor does it give me any clues as to why the war lives on here.

We speed home in a driving squall. We're drenched in thirty seconds. I'd forgotten how cold tropical rain can be, and I recall Robert Leckie's war memoir, *Helmet for My Pillow*: "The rainy season was upon us . . . whole days of downpour when I lay drenched and shivering, gazing blankly out of my hole, watching as the sheeted gray rain whipped and undulated over the Ridge. At such times, a man's brain seems to cease to function . . . one is aware only of life, of wetness, of the cold gray rain."

En route back to Ughele, benumbed by the rain, my mind takes me back to the war, back to my earlier stay in the Solomons.

In 1977, before we moved to Honiara, the Solomons to me meant Guadalcanal—an old newsreel of exhausted Leathernecks slogging single file like pack mules through steamy jungle; Sherman tanks foundering in hip-deep mud; John Wayne rallying his men for another assault. Like *Victory at Sea*, Guadalcanal seemed a faded video, an era long gone—my father's generation.

I realized quickly World War II hadn't faded away. Guadalcanal was a great game park, inhabited not by the wildebeests and lions of Africa, but by rusting hulks of the predators of war.

It's 1978. Machete in hand, I slash my way three meters off a path in the jungle. A crumpled fighter plane leers from its vine-woven mausoleum. From the movies, I had a more dramatic image: a P-38 dives into battle, guns blazing. It twists, turns, eludes the enemy, pursues him. Telltale smoke puffs out. Another Zero flames into the sea. (We always won in those movie dogfights. In the real-life Guadalcanal campaign, America lost 615 planes; the Japanese, 682.)

But this relic suffers no bullet holes, no fire-scarred engine, no blasted wing. This pilot simply didn't make it back to Henderson Field. Did he run out of fuel? Did some makeshift part fail? I imagine the downed pilot, led by Jacob Vouza, creeping back through Japanese lines, returning to battle in another craft.

Mid-1979: I'm trudging through chest-high *nila* grass (needle grass—it can shred pants) down the side of a ridge above Henderson Field, trying to find a path to the Lungga River. Suddenly, I'm face to face with an unexploded bomb. I inch away on cat's paws.

Early 1980: Heaped shell casings and rotted C-ration cans like shabby grave markers lead me to a GI foxhole on Bloody Ridge overlooking Henderson Field. I jump in, imagine mortars honing in, machine-gun fire.

John Hersey joined the Marines' H Company on Guadalcanal in 1942. They hiked this ridge. He writes in *Into the Valley*: "The first thing a green man fixes upon in his mind is the noise . . . . Its constant fabric was rifle fire . . . like a knife tearing into the fabric . . . . The noise of the mortars was . . . a thump which vibrated not just your eardrums, but your entrails as well . . . dive bombs fumbling into the jungle, the laughter of strafing P-39s . . . the soft, fluttery noise of our artillery shells making a trip. The noise alone was enough to scare a new man . . . ."

November 1991: Before coming to Ughele, I spend a month in Honiara. On a hot, lazy Sunday, thudding explosions like echoes from long-departed American guns jolt me back into my father's war. Wartime puffs of smoke curl over Bloody Ridge like a smoke signal from history.

Fifty years after America liberated the Solomons, torrential rains still flush bombs from their tombs. Scorching sun bakes them. They erode in tropical cycles of heat and rain. Errant movement—a city crew digging, a slash-and-burn farmer plowing with a sharpened stick, a child exploring—or age alone detonates them. That long-ago war lives on, even in the new century.

Between mid-1988 and mid-1991, demolition teams exploded more than forty thousand bombs in the Solomons. The head of the nation's bomb disposal unit noted in 1989, "Hell's Point [an ammunition dump near the airport] alone will take twenty to twenty-five years to clear."

Today's incessant rain, this freezing torrential downpour, reminds me that only death or rain can quiet the noise of battle. I think of Robert Leckie and John Hersey in those Guadalcanal foxholes, buried to their thighs in muck. A foxhole can easily become a boggy crypt.

For the Allies, Guadalcanal marked a turning point: victory here put the Allies on the offense. To Solomon Islanders, it brought both liberation and the beginning of monumental changes in their country and their traditional way of life.

The Solomon Islands capital city of Honiara didn't exist on August 7, 1942, when the First Marine Division splashed ashore near Point Cruz. Marines swept past sleepy clusters of thatched huts, now swallowed up by Honiara—Tasimboko, Mataniko, Kukum. They captured a Japanese airstrip and named it Henderson Field to honor an American pilot shot down over Midway Island. They bivouacked in coconut plantations and at jungle's edge.

For months America clung to Henderson as the Japanese clawed at its perimeter. Daily bombing and nightly shelling threatened a tenuous hold. Rain, steamy heat, malaria, and dysentery battered both armies. The battle dragged on for six months. It ended in February 1943, when Japan withdrew 10,652 debilitated, starving men from Cape Esperance, twenty-one miles west of Point Cruz. More than seven thousand Americans and thirty thousand Japanese died fighting for Guadalcanal. Allied victory ended Japan's unimpeded advance on Australia. From here, war in the Pacific marched slowly northward—first to Rendova and New Georgia, then beyond the Solomons to Rabaul, Tarawa, Guam, Iwo Jima, Okinawa, and finally, in 1945, to Nagasaki and Hiroshima.

On the long ride from Lumberia Island to Ughele, the immediacy of Chief Willie's war stories intrigues me. Ughele has no violence—and thus no jail—no reason for war to live on in the nightly storytelling. Unless even pastoral men need a daily shot of violence, much like we Americans need the evening news and our action movies, to remind them peace is preferable to war. Maybe it's that tales of individual daring and cataclysmic battles thrive in oral history. After all, raids by pre-Christian headhunters, confrontations with missionaries, and clashes with British colonials also live on in the nightly stories. In an oral society, history has no newspapers, no library archives. It breathes anew with each day's retelling.

Solomon Islanders believe themselves uniquely tied by the war to America. The feeling isn't mutual. Unlike residents of other US battlegrounds in Europe, Japan, Korea, Vietnam, and the Philippines, Solomon Islanders never entered America's continuing consciousness. We never bonded through massive post-war occupation or aid, through immigration or intermarriage.

In America, the Solomons' war is no more than a bittersweet memory. For those who fought there, war may merit occasional reflection, like thumbing through an old photo album, then consigning it again to the mementos box. For those whose only tie is a father—or now, grandfather—who fought there, of what meaning is today's Solomons?

My generation's war was Vietnam, but I'm a conscientious objector. I should be repulsed by Chief Willie's stories, but, somehow, they fascinate me. It's a dissonance that grew, ironically, from my Peace Corps service. As a volunteer in the mid-'60s, I taught in Tacloban City, Leyte—near where Gen. Douglas MacArthur, keeping his promise of "I shall return," returned to the Philippines. Two of my fellow teachers survived the Bataan Death March and the prison camp horrors that followed. In the US, we recount the atrocities in terms of the 11,500 Americans captured on Bataan. We Americans forget—or never knew—that 65,000 Filipinos suffered the same fate. My co-workers' anecdotes brought that infamous story to life.

In the late '70s, while living on Guadalcanal, my wife and I also supervised volunteers in the Gilbert Islands. I spent many a day on Tarawa, site of a bloody Marine landing.

Good men died in all those places. Others survived unspeakable horrors. One thing's clear: one doesn't dishonor pacifism by honoring the individual courage that war demands.

World War II liberated the Solomons and the Gilberts from Japanese oppression and paved the way for the death of British colonialism. Thus, I, too, sent money to the Guadalcanal-Solomon Islands War Memorial Foundation. Today, tourists can visit official war sites, as well as battlefield remnants on Guadalcanal: a granite and marble American memorial on Skyline Ridge, a larger-than-life bronze at Rove police station of Sir Jacob Vouza, a US memorial on Bloody Ridge, and the rebuilt wooden control tower that peers over Henderson Airport like a 1940s forest-fire tower. All were dedicated in three busy days beginning August 7, 1992, exactly fifty years after the US Marine landing.

Perhaps these physical memorials will give a few wandering Americans a new sense of their own history, or an inkling of how profoundly another nation holds America in its memory.

In Ughele, I come to envy Chief Willie's living memories of his father, who has been dead for several years. My father, too, fought in World War II, but he wasn't a storyteller. He died in a car accident in 1961, killed by a drunk driver. He never said a word about the war, not to his four kids. The Marshall family has no war stories.

We have a photo of Dad's H Company, 255th Infantry, taken in basic training at Fort Hood, Texas. He sailed from New York on November 25, 1944—my third birthday. Two weeks later, on December 8, he landed at Marseille, one more private in the 63rd Division, Seventh Army.

My father printed his personal war history neatly on a single "service record" page in the Armed Services Memorial Edition of Miller's *The Complete History of World War II*, as if the book were the family Bible. He left the briefest of records:

"Committed (to battle) Dec 23, 44.

"Entered Germany, Mar 15, 45.

"125 consecutive days on line.

"Relieved at 20 km from Munich, May 7.

"War ended in Germany.

"Sailed from Bremer Haven, Germany 12 Mar 46. Arrived N.Y. 23 Mar 46 aboard U.S.S. Victory Eufala. Released from service April 1, 1946, Ft. Lewis, Wash."

The Solomons campaign had ended long before PFC Charles Homer Marshall sailed for Europe. In the Pacific, Saipan and Guam had fallen. American B-29s had bombed Tokyo.

Gen. Alexander Patch, commander on Guadalcanal when the Japanese fled in February 1943, now commanded America's Seventh Army in France, one component of a massive multi-fronted push through the winter of 1944–45 into Germany. My father joined Patch's command two days before Christmas 1944 as the Battle of the Bulge raged to the north of Patch's troops.

Chief Willie's father, in loincloth and with captured Japanese weapons, fought in the jungle forest of his homeland. Through his son, his war exploits live on.

My father? His story must be imagined, conjured up from the reams that detail the sweep into Germany that bitter winter. Besides Miller's *History*, my father left his family a Veterans of Foreign Wars book, *Pictorial History of World War II*, and Bill Mauldin's *Up Front*.

Germany surrendered on May 8, 1945, but my father remained there for nearly a year. Did he, like Col. George Tuck on Guadalcanal, take time to meet the "natives," to fashion a bit of the familiar out of the alien environment into which he had been thrust?

I'll never know. Chief Willie's canoe took me only as far as Lumberia and Munda, into the Pacific war. Germany lies beyond a different ocean. I suspect my father's war was more akin to that of Bill Mauldin's Willie and Joe than to Chief Willie's stories. Maybe we don't need an oral account to keep my father's war alive. He left us Mauldin's cartoons.

On another sleepless night in Ughele, I struggle to reconcile my mishmash of images. War transformed the Solomons, even remote Rendova. Tens of thousands of troops swarmed islands occupied by tens, or at most, a few hundred villagers. Giant machines carved roads. Vehicles belched across the islands. Hundreds of islanders poured into Guadalcanal to work as stevedores and laborers. A city sprouted. Goods flowed. The invasion trampled existing social patterns.

American soldiers discovered that war, even on bloody Guadalcanal, could be other than one deadly charge after another into the breach. Some soldiers manned desks. They requisitioned provisions, cut orders, drafted reports. Others cooked meals, built roads, hauled supplies, handled mail or repaired planes and tanks and Jeeps. Like George Tuck, they played basketball, explored, tended gardens, jawed for hours over homemade hooch, and shot craps. They befriended Solomon Islanders, gave them food and clothing, and exchanged stories and trinkets.

During World War II, American soldiers saw precious few women in the Solomons. Most were safely hidden in the hills. GIs took no wives from the Solomons, visited no prostitutes, left behind no children—as they did in Australia and New Zealand, on the European front, in Japan, Okinawa, Guam, the Philippines, later Korea, Vietnam, Thailand, the Philippines again. Maybe that's one reason Solomon Islanders so openly welcome Americans.

Jonathan Fifi'i, a Solomon Islander who worked in the labor corps on Guadalcanal, recalls in *The Big Death: Solomon Islanders Remember World War II* his first impressions of Americans: "They asked us to come inside their houses . . . what they called 'tents.' Big pieces of canvas. They invited us inside, and when we were inside, we could sit on their beds. We got inside and they gave us their glasses so we could drink out of them too. They gave us plates and we ate with their own spoons. This was the first we had seen of that kind of thing."

Early in 1943, black American soldiers landed on Guadalcanal. Many were laborers, but some black units went on to fight in New Georgia. They left an indelible heritage. Fifi'i writes: "Our bodies were the same. Some of them were really black, just like the people from Choiseul and the people from the Shortland Islands . . . . But regardless, they were really great people! Any kind of thing that the whites did, they could do it too. They knew how to do carpentry, and they knew how to write. And they were the people that we worked together with."

Fifi'i spent three years in prison after the war for "acts of sedition"—he sought to organize his people against colonial domination—then went on to become a member of the Solomon Islands parliament. Many Solomon Islanders resented British rule before the war, but it was the war that galvanized them. Fifi'i recalls how Americans encouraged him: "They told us, 'If you do it, they will lock you up in jail, they will tie you up, they'll shoot you. But you can't be afraid because you're strong. You must stand up and look them in the eye, be strong and big, and break the ties holding you to the whites. That's what we are telling you.' And we were not afraid, and we did it."

Thirty-five years later, in 1978, Fifi'i took me to a meeting of headmen of the isolated Kwaio, the last pagan tribe in the Solomons, in the mountains of his native Malatia. He wanted Peace Corps volunteers to help run a new Kwaio culture center, but the Kwaio made such decisions only by consensus. We negotiated in a leaf hut near their proposed site. The elders filled the hut, three dozen bare-chested, sinewy mountain men in loin cloths, hunkering on the dirt floor, puffing homemade pipes. I spoke Pijin; Jonathan translated into Kwaio. They grilled me: "What will they do, these Peace Corps?" one man asked. Others chimed in: "What do they eat? Will they live in a Kwaio house? Must we pay them? We have no money."

For three hours we met, rehashing some questions five times. Finally, one old man stood, and announced in Kwaio, "We do not understand this Peace Corps. But you represent America, not Britain. We trust you. We want a Peace Corps."

Chief Willie knows his Solomon Islands war history. He knows also how deceptive the peace and quiet of village life can be—especially on Rendova. He realizes a new era of change confronts Ughele, and all Solomons.

No multinationals tend coconut plantations on Rendova. It has no tuna cannery, no gold mine, no government center. But virgin rainforest covers the island. Logging flourishes. By late December, in my fourth week in Ughele, the discordant snarls of bulldozer and chainsaw shatter the silence. "Progress" chews a road closer and closer to the village.

On New Year's Eve, at the home of a local big-man, I meet a Chinese-Malaysian who manages the logging company. He will extend the new logging road through the village. "We will rebuild Ughele," he boasts. New Ughele will be a modern town, laid out neatly in rows. The old, familiar huts will be lost, yes, but corrugated iron and lumber last longer than thatch, and they are more handsome, he tells me.

Two days into 1992, trees topple in the jungle behind the school. The logging company will carve a new soccer field for the kids, Chief Willie promises. He doesn't mention the road.

Ughele earns a royalty payment for each tree logged. Every village member, from child to adult, owns an equal share. The village has bought its own ship from Japan—not a small boat, but an inter-island cargo ship. It will ply the Western Solomons, exporting logs and importing supplies to Ughele and neighboring islands, mining logging royalties for further profit.

A Solomon Islands' crew has flown to Japan to sail the ship to the Solomons. Each night Pastor tracks its progress on a short-wave radio. It will be here by Christmas, he reports. Then, New Year's. Rough seas, further delay: mid-January.

Even in conservative Ughele, age-old prohibitions seem under attack. Willie had explained local beliefs so we visitors wouldn't violate custom: no alcohol, public smoking, or pre-marital sex. A holy Sabbath, modest dress, late-night quiet.

But at Christmas, youths flock home, some from school, others from jobs or from hanging out in Honiara. Teenagers roam till dawn. They flaunt accoutrements of the city: gaudy T-shirts, sunglasses, and short skirts. And though most Solomon Islanders go barefoot, a few youths sport athletic shoes. They swap cassettes and with battery-run boom boxes, assault the village with the ear-splitting cacophony my preteen son hammers me with in Denver. All night *sing-sings* assail our sleep. Cigarette butts—some bearing lipstick stains—smolder along the main path.

No one sells liquor in Ughele, but in the wee hours, across the footbridge to Kombi, a barrio at one end of the village, traveled young men sing in drunken revelry. A few daring girls join them. Beer comes from Munda or Noro, where construction of a tuna cannery has produced a boom town. In calm sea, either source is four hours roundtrip by motorized canoe.

A Saturday stroll catches backsliders at home rather than in church, wash being laid out to dry, cooking fires burning. One of Willie's teenage daughters asks if I want her to find a village woman to sleep with me. A local girl has moved in with a Peace Corps stud.

Chief Willie overlooks the transgressions. They're too prevalent, and he knows no village sea wall can keep them out. Change is part of Solomon Islands history. He chooses to work with it, to try to nudge it in directions that foster his vision of the future.

Over the years, correspondence with friends in the Solomons fades away. In her last letter, one friend writes in 1995, "Things are well in Honiara. I hear nothing of Ughele." By chance my wife and daughter meet a Solomon Islander in Hawaii in 2001. He still sends an occasional email. He has a job, and doesn't plan to go home: the economy's failing, the opportunities few. He's right. Government mismanagement and corruption are rampant. As the economy declined, so did relations between the many Malaitans on Guadalcanal, and Guadalcanal natives. Skirmishes broke out in the late 1990s, then escalated into armed battles between the Malaita Eagle Force and the Istabu Freedom Movement. In June 2000, a coup d'état overthrew the government.

The root cause: Honiara's mushrooming growth. Founded at Point Cruz in 1942, it has grown to 45,498, a tenth of the country's population. (The second largest city in the country is Gizo, population 5,984.) Islanders swarmed into the capital city—most of them Malaitans—took jobs in government and private industry, bought up and/or squatted on traditional lands.

The twenty-first century saw armed ruffians terrorize Honiara—stores looted, innocents accosted, robbed, beaten, several murdered. Thousands of Malaitans left to their home island. Expats fled. The export industries—palm oil, copra, logging, tuna fishing and canning—screeched to a halt. Local businesses closed. Tourism died out. National debt skyrocketed. The Peace Corps withdrew its volunteers in June 2000. They have not returned.

The warring parties signed a peace accord in October 2000 and the nation regained a modicum of order, but violence continued. Several government men were assassinated. In July 2003, Australia sent in a force of 1,750 troops to help local police restore law and order: the first influx of foreign soldiers into the Solomons since World War II. An additional five hundred men from Fiji, Tonga, New Zealand and Papua New Guinea joined them.

In August 2003, as if to reinforce Guadalcanal's image of a land facing never-ending war, workers discovered a World War II cache of more than one hundred live 75 mm shells in central Honiara. Three years later, in April 2006, violence erupted again: rioters burned Honiara's Chinatown business district to the ground. More than a thousand Chinese, many of them lifetime residents, fled the country. As of January 2007, Aussie occupation continues, supplemented by a contingent of expat civil servants trying to revamp the corruption-plagued ministries.

Law and order have been restored. The economy is recovering. But logging—now fifty percent of the nation's exports—far outpaces reforestation and threatens the delicate ecosystem.

In the capital city, tension mounts between Solomon Islanders and Aussies. In September 2006, the prime minister declared the Australian high commissioner (ambassador) *persona non grata* and expelled him for meddling in local politics. Islanders grumble about high-living Aussies. Prostitution has increased. A January 2007 email from the Honiara Society for Outing Unfaithful Expatriates announced its intent to eliminate marital infidelity by expat ministry officials living in Honiara.

In Ughele? Who knows. Ughele has no email, no newspaper. Australia says the danger lies in Honiara and rural Guadalcanal. It warns its citizens to defer travel to the Solomons. That means everywhere: all legal access to the Solomons begins in Honiara.

I suspect life goes on in Ughele much as before. Residents grow their own food, catch fish, rebuild their houses with thatch and handmade twine. This new war, this civil war, becomes another topic in the nightly *tok-tok*, mixed with weather prospects, local gossip, tales from before.

I imagine Chief Willie shaking his head, wondering about the men of Guadalcanal and Malaita. "That's life in Solomon Islands," he might say. "War remains always with us."

Guantanamera
KATIE ROSE GUEST

1. My sister told me, "Buy the shoes a size too small. The leather stretches when you dance, from the sweat." At the dancewear shop, I slip on a gold T-strap sandal with a low Cuban heel. I stand and feel the stiff leather cut my ankle and instep as my foot arches. But the suede sole grips the linoleum floor, and I think how my mambo will be so sweet, one-*two*-three-four. I pay sixty dollars for the shoes and throw them in the seat next to me in my car. I sing with Celia Cruz on the stereo as I drive away, *Guantanamera . . . guajira Guantanamera*.

2. *One, two, three, four*. The young girl counts the men standing on the big wall far in the distance. Her mother doesn't like her to come here, but she sneaks away sometimes. Like everyone who lives near this place, she is careful to step around the dull metal things on the ground, feeling with her bare feet when she walks. The men on the wall don't look like men to her, just tall dark blocks against the sun. She knows they're men only because one day she sat on the hill on a smooth rock, for hours and hours she thought, until she almost fell asleep. She watched until finally the dark shadows on the wall moved and were replaced by new dark shadows that looked just as not-human, just as still.

3. The soldier knows something is wrong even before he looks through the bars. The cell is too still. After years at this post he has learned that even when a prisoner is sleeping the air in a cell moves with the vibrations of life. He thinks about all of the life caught inside this massive hornet's nest. Each chamber is hollowed out and filled with captured prey, then patched over to trap the prey inside and hide it from those outside—from the ones who might poach or steal it away. *It's amazing*, he thinks, as he finally makes out the man's body hanging in the shadows, eyes rolled back in his head to give a ghastly white glare, *this hasn't happened sooner*.

Along the Camino de Santiago
Jacqueline Kolosov

Cuando la vida no pesa, es possible vivir.
—Mario Benedetti

In Spanish, the word for pilgrim is *peregrino*, though this is not its only meaning. *Peregrino* is also strange and absurd as well as fleeting, transitory. Strange and absurd made sense to me, for a pilgrim had to be a little weird to choose the blisters, leg pain, and cumulative fatigue that inevitably accompanied days of walking in the hot Spanish sun. But fleeting? This other meaning, I decided, would take time to reveal itself.

Onward, from the jewel-like St. Jean Pied-de-Port through Roncesvalles I walked, immediately grateful for the gentle curves of the Pyrenees, and the mild temperatures. To guide me, a yellow scallop shell, the official sign of the pilgrim, adorned trees, telephone poles, even the corners of buildings.

Six days into a pilgrimage I had begun on a remarkably mild first day of August, I left the mountains for the softer rise and fall of Navarre. It was outside the village of Estella that I misread one of the yellow signs and wound up straying a good eight kilometers from the Camino before realizing that I was heading east, back into the mountains, instead of west toward Santiago.

According to the medievals, the pilgrim shed her former self en route to Santiago, the sins or at least the baggage vanishing with the sweat and excess pounds. By walking west, a person walked out of herself. The old self must die for the new self to be born, the *Compostela* said.

And what did I need to shed? The tear-streaked face of the twenty-four-year-old woman who stood before a candlelit altar at the university chapel and vowed to love, honor, and cherish Ian—a man I had met during my first year of college—*until death do us part.* Ian, a man who had walked with me through the Alps of Austria; but also a man who had become someone strange to me, someone in whom I could no longer recognize my own face. *Until death do us part.*

By the time I reached the *auberge* (pilgrim's hostel) in the village of Viana, it was pitch dark. The dinner had already been served, and there were no leftovers. As for the beds, each and every one had been claimed. My *faulta* meant that I had to dine on a gristly hunk of cheese and some hard bread. Worse yet, my only sleeping option became a tent with three Spaniards, all of whom were named Jesus and all of whom snored.

Getting lost was one of my problems, but it wasn't the only one. Although the Outward Bound salesperson had sold me a superb pair of featherweight boots before I left Chicago, blisters cropped up on my toes. These I treated nightly, alongside the other pilgrims, bending over my feet, as if in prayer, as I applied the trademark slick white ointment.

Eight days later, in the town of Fromista, I failed to make the traditional early start. True, my feet ached, and new blisters had begun to bubble over the old ones that still had not healed.

Yet foot pain was not the only reason for my slowness. That morning I felt especially lazy, and there was a dull ache in my low back. With the hot Spanish sun beating down, I actually began to contemplate blowing my Santiago savings by checking into a chic hotel, or any hotel for that matter (Fromista was not a glamorous place), where I could spend the day soaking in a hot bath, then settling into the cool, clean whiteness of cotton sheets.

Such subversion was the reason why 11:00 a.m. found me sitting at an outdoor café in a cobblestone plaza, drinking my third café con leche and gobbling pastry as gray pigeons scouted for crumbs beneath my feet.

Into this tranquil scene stepped Mariano Guitierez, his brown cheeks flushed with sweat, his enormous smile just preceding his throbbing baritone voice. "It's the lovely American! My god, what are you doing here?"

Not only me but every other person at the café looked up to spot the husky Venezuelan, the two signature steel ski poles he used to walk the Camino clutched in his hands, his exceptionally white socks standing out in bold relief against his toffee skin.

Mariano slid into the chair opposite me, his black hair damp beneath the Dunlop baseball cap he wore backwards, the strap just above his one long eyebrow. As he reached for my water glass and took a long, deep swallow, I recalled his first words one hot night near Pamplona. "I want to live the Camino as they did in the Middle Ages. Alone. Like a real pilgrim."

Despite his earlier declaration, that morning dressed in a sweaty red T-shirt that said, "Caracas is for Lovers," a silver earring piercing his left lobe, a stainless-steel wristwatch strapped to his tanned wrist, Mariano looked thoroughly modern and perhaps even a little dangerous. In fact, there were those pilgrims who speculated that the handsome Venezuelan who claimed to be studying philology in Cologne was in reality a terrorist.

"Tell me, lovely—"

"Jacqueline—"

"*Jacqueline*, of course, a name like a village in the south of France." He leaned closer. "*Tell me*, why aren't you walking?"

Over yet another café con leche, I explained my various travails.

"Hard luck," he considered, biting into my sticky bun. "Still, such things are to be expected during a holy year."

I frowned.

"You know what I think?" Mariano asked.

Certain that fellow feeling was on its way, especially given his free way with my sticky buns, I leaned forward. "What?"

"I think you're not a real pilgrim."

"If I'm not a real pilgrim," I said, "then you aren't one either."

Mariano drew himself up very straight, crumbs from the chocolate bun he had just devoured sticking to the edges of his mouth. "Of course I am a real pilgrim. I have the *tendoneetis* to prove it."

"Tendonitis or not, you're still sitting in a café eating chocolate buns and harassing me."

Mariano opened his box of a mouth and laughed. "You know what?" he said coyly. "I think you're glad to see me."

Close to two hours later, once Mariano had eaten yet another chocolate bun (this one his own), and once I had purchased a thick, new pair of microfiber, sweat-wicking socks (at Mariano's recommendation), we resumed walking.

Though the terrain was flat and easygoing, because of our late start we did not reach the next *auberge* until after eight. By this time, the other pilgrims had already showered, eaten, and claimed all the beds.

Still, Mariano managed to charm the *hospitalera* into finding a bunk for me and one for himself. "I also convinced her to let us have hot water. We can have a shower."

Although his native tongue was not English, I wondered at these constant slippages. Besides, as I stooped to untie my boots, I was aware of the fact that he was looking down my shirt. "You have lovely breasts," he said, and then, before the words had time to register, "Can I borrow your soap?"

As I dug beneath T-shirts and underwear and a canvas bag full of maps and papers, Mariano exclaimed, "My God, what a disaster. It's time you learned how to pack your *muchilla* [rucksack]."

I narrowed my eyes and fought back my smile as I said, "Go to hell."

Mariano just leaned back and laughed.

As was to be expected, privacy on the Camino was minimal and modesty impossible, for many *auberges* possessed only a single toilet and shower. Crowded side by side in steep bunk beds or in sleeping bags on the floor, people quickly found out who snored, who talked in his sleep, as well as who dared to have sex in a room full of slumbering *peregrinos* with sore feet and sunburns.

Despite the foot pain and other small hardships, the blissful monotony of walking all day in a slowly changing landscape transfigured by light and shadow created a subtle yet radically altered sense of time. Past and future lost their meaning. There was only an endless present, a *now* so dense the moments overflowed. One became just a figure in a landscape. Walking.

As I walked, what I perceived as the momentousness of my own history, the fact that I had not been able to stay with Ian, whom I cared for but to whom I could no longer belong, ceased to overwhelm me. Though I did not know if this new way of seeing was a *milagro* (miracle), I was grateful for the new sense of peace.

Another unexpected source of, not peace exactly, but companionship, was Mariano, with whom I spent more than a week, joking, fighting, and talking. Not only did he share my love of literature and music and history, not only could he narrate a story with such embellishment that it could stretch out over the course of several miles of walking; but he shared my inexplicable need to explore the why between so many aspects of existence, from the infinite potential of love within all of us to its simultaneous finiteness within the course of a single relationship. After all, Mariano had parted from his own first wife. And I had parted from Ian.

And yet, Mariano was remarkably more lighthearted than me and often opened his wide box of a mouth and said, "Jacqueline, you need to take life less seriously."

At such times, I almost began to believe that Mariano had been sent to help me walk the Camino, though I could not possibly consider the opinionated although endearing Venezuelan a *milagro*. Still—

Once, after climbing a rugged mountain path leading to the twelfth century village of O'Cebrero, I unlaced my boots only to discover that my right ankle had swelled to nearly twice its size.

"*Cariña*," Mariano said, patiently removing the sock, then massaging the sore muscles with the medicinal lotion he used to treat his own tendonitis.

With my foot resting in Mariano's lap, I felt as if no one had ever treated me so well. Of course, this was absurd. Still, at that moment, I felt absolutely safe. As for my ankle, by morning the swelling was gone, and I was able to continue walking.

Two mornings later, Mariano ran a finger back and forth across his long eyebrow and said, "We have been spending so much time together lately. I need to walk alone for a while."

"You want to separate?" I asked.

"We're sure to meet up again in one hundred kilometers or so."

When I did not reply, Mariano fished around in his rucksack for the little headset he frequently listened to. "Here," he said, "hold onto this. If we don't meet beforehand, when you come into Galicia, play this music. Will you?"

"Okay," I said, well aware of the gift's significance, for Mariano always spoke of playing this particular piece of Celtic music when he reached Galicia's fabled mountains.

Nevertheless, when Mariano reached out to touch me, a sign of intimacy radically unlike our easier flirtatious bantering and distinctly intellectual exchanges, I pulled away, strangely reminded of the last time I saw Ian. We were leaving the courtroom, Ian ahead of me, walking fast. I had called after him to wait, then watched as he continued moving farther and farther away. "Ian," I'd cried. "Ian."

Not once did he turn around.

"I'm sorry, Jacqueline," Ian wrote a few days later. "You just can't have it both ways. For me, friendship with you is impossible."

Two days after parting from Mariano, I made my way up a narrow, root-trammeled path. Having started out very early, I'd had the path entirely to myself, the trees and the birds and the sun my only companions.

Suddenly, I heard someone calling out to me.

About twenty feet ahead, partially hidden beneath the shade of a tree, sat a lovely woman somewhere in her fifties. The woman's eyes were large and hazel-colored, her hair a silvery-blond.

"Do you need some help?" I asked.

"I need some water," the woman said. "I seem to have drained my canteen."

I handed the woman my own bottle, and pretty soon we found ourselves sitting side by side, our hiking boots unlaced so that our feet could breathe.

Over a repast of melting chocolate and apricots, Erica Bauer told me that she had come to Spain from Brazil. From the diamonds in Erica's ears and the exquisite weave of her silk walking clothes, I sensed that Erica's life was strictly upper class, a feeling confirmed by Erica's confession that her family owned one of the country's largest steel factories. They spent holidays in a series of villas along the coast.

Erica went on to share her history, telling me of the husband she loved, a man she found it impossible to live with and without. "Jaime is man who does not know how to be faithful," Erica confided, relaying this truth as if it were just a fact with which she had to live (which I supposed it was).

After discussing each of her four children, all of whom had begun families of their own, and one of whom had placed twice in the equestrienne division of the last Olympics, she said, "But enough about me. Tell me about you."

So I did. As we walked to the next village some fifteen kilometers away, I confided Ian's problems with manic depression, my own problems sleeping, the panic attacks, the divorce that eventually followed. To no one else had I said as much about all that had happened. "The thing is," I continued, "sometimes I'm afraid of what I've done."

Erica's large eyes rested calmly on my face. "What is the worst thing that could happen?" When I didn't answer, Erica said, "Well?"

"I'll wind up alone."

"But darling," Erica said, a radiant smile dawning, "you were alone when you met me."

I walked with Erica for two days. Three days after we parted, I entered the fabled emerald mountains of Galicia. Galicia, the word was itself a melody. Even the villages possessed musical names that rang with the jeweled lightness of cowbells: Fonfria, Filoval, San Gil, and Barbadelo. Here, houses were built of shining golden stone. There were flower boxes beneath the windows and brightly painted doors. Friendly, flea-infested dogs roamed every street, lithe cats drowsed in sun spots beneath open doorways, and cows went where and did what they pleased.

With the sun warming my skin and bones, I lay down in the high, sweet grass and opened my eyes to the azure sky overhead. I placed Mariano's headset over my ears and turned on the tape player. The music felt like the sunlight on my back and the salt taste of my warm skin. It became the new strength in my shoulders and in my thighs, the scent of peaches ripening in the sun, the shadows of the fragrant eucalyptus trees.

Listening, I heard the children running through a plaza in Astorga. They were there within me, laughing and out of breath, tiny red flags in their hands, as they rushed toward an ice cream vendor pushing an old-fashioned aluminum cart. Here again were the shaggy dogs mating in an amber field as an old shepherd slept beneath the olive trees surrounded by dozens of woolly sheep. So many sensuous images flooded my body, the music carrying me along on an electric current, until I felt as if I had stepped out of myself.

The next day, I reached the village of Mellide, which marked the end of Galicia and the onset of *Coruña,* the last region in Spain and home to the fabled city of Santiago. I found the village ablaze with color, each lamppost adorned with papery flags of pink and gold. Everywhere, voices rang out amidst the joyful confusion of street vendors, honking automobiles, and barking dogs. Mesmerized, I stood there, trying to soak it all in, until a bearded priest approached me. "Are you a *peregrina?"* he asked.

When I said yes, the priest invited me to join in the celebration at the local restaurant. "You have never had *pulpo* [octopus] prepared the way we do it in Mellide, and *empañada con bonitos* [fish pie], and *vino tinto* [red wine]."

For two hours, I joined in the revelry. Parents introduced me to their children. A sexy, forty-year-old widower winked and told me to "come and find me" if I ever wanted to settle down. One woman even gave me a tiny bronze icon, a sort of good luck charm.

Afterwards, drunk on the *vino tinto* and drowsy from the large meal, I found that I could not continue walking, especially not in the heat of the two o'clock sun. So I lay down, choosing as my resting place a grassy hillside beneath a fig tree. Above my head, the fruit ripened in the summer heat, the soft green skin just touched with a rich shade of purple brown.

Beside the fig tree stood a post emblazoned with the symbolic scallop shell. Every once in a while, other pilgrims reached the post only to find me sprawled out on the lumpy earth. Antonio, the historian from Sevilla, was among the first. Later the chic, brown Frenchwoman who always wore white arrived, her skin browner and her clothes whiter than ever. Even the bespectacled German organist and her Basque lover turned up close to dusk, sun-browned, their hands entwined, their bodies lit from within.

Inevitably, the proximity to Santiago, as well as the stream of familiar faces, reminded me that my time in Spain was drawing to a close. Would I see Mariano again?

"If I come into Santiago," Mariano always began, dark eyes shining, for arrival always existed as a possibility and not as a certainty in his mind. Mariano had undertaken the pilgrimage to prove to himself that he could see something difficult all the way through from start to finish. "If I come into Santiago, I will buy a pair of new shoes for my poor, destroyed feet. From there, I will walk to the cathedral. Afterwards, I will dance in the streets."

I thought of Mariano, but I also thought about Ian who had always spoken of seeing Spain's famous cities and well-known historic places: Guernica; the Alhambra, the Prado Museum in Madrid with its cache of paintings by Goya, Velazquez, and El Greco. The Spain I now knew was not Ian's Spain at all.

I did not reach the *auberge* until after dark. By the time I arrived, it had begun to rain. A grim-faced *hospitelero* told me that there was no longer any room in the main dormitory.

"What about the tents?" I asked.

The *hospitalero* just shook his head. "You're better off sleeping outside. The tents are infested with fleas."

Accustomed to the travails of the pilgrim by now, I shrugged, then headed off in the direction of the *auberge*'s open porch. Shaded by some old trees, the porch looked cool and inviting.

I could just make out the outline of a sleeping bag already on the floor. No matter, I thought, removing my *muchilla*, then taking out what I needed for the night.

"My God," a familiar voice called out. "Jacqueline, is that really you?"

I looked up to see Mariano, hair wet with rain, dark skin glistening, box smile huge and more than a little radiant.

The next thing I knew, we were in each other's arms.

"There's so much I want to tell you," I said, as we sat together in the cool silence, the only sound the rustle of the green-leafed branches.

"We will have plenty of time for talking," Mariano said. "Now we will be able to walk into the city of Santiago together. We will be able to dance in the streets, our blistered feet beautiful because of our journey."

A few weeks, possibly even a few days ago, I would have accepted Mariano's words without question.

"What is it?" he asked, turning to me.

"I'm sorry," I heard myself say. "I can't walk with you."

Mariano laughed. "You can't be serious."

Thinking of my days with Erica, my solitary ascent through Galicia, the feast in Mellide, but thinking also of the reason I had come to Spain, the absolute need to shed the self who had clung to Ian long after the love between us had died. I stared into Mariano's night-dark eyes and said, "I don't think I understood until now, but I need to come into the city alone."

Mariano did not protest. Yet he held me even closer after that.

In the morning, long before the sun came up, I dressed, re-packed my *muchilla*, then stood on the chilly terrace looking down at my friend's long body curled in sleep. Very gently, I stooped to kiss Mariano's tanned brow.

As I made my way down the hill to find the Camino, I started walking, my own breath difficult, my thoughts unfocused. But after an hour or so, my breathing softened, and I felt my hips lean into the path. And little by little, the tight knot of my self washed away. Until there was nothing left but the walking, the road, the earth, the sky.

A Prayer for My Daughter, Who Does Not Exist
Dan Albergotti

Bless you, my hollow child, lying under nothing tonight
in one of those other worlds. Let there be wind, for there is
no wind. Let me hear it and fear nothing for you.

Bless your yawning, unreal mouth, your even breath.
When you wake, will your first word be *Daddy*
or *God*? Let it be *God*, let there be that.

Bless your tiny fingers playing on my face, in my hair,
under my skull. Let there be your soft touch, for there is
no touch. And let there be the light crescent moons of your nails.

Bless everything you will do and all your dreams.
Dream of your father. Dream of your god. Let there be
years and years and years, for there is no future.

And since between each world there is nothing,
let there be a prayer. Let me bless your too-pale skin,
your too-auburn hair, your beautiful impossibility.

The Pond
Jonatha Ceely

After the husband retired from the investment firm in the city and the wife from the suburban medical practice where she was the claims manager, the couple established a new habit of walking for an hour every morning. Life would be healthier for them now, they agreed. He no longer rushed to board the train that trundled commuters through grimy yards, past storage sheds, along weed-grown rights of way. She no longer hurried, tense behind the wheel, to claim a convenient parking place near the sprawling, red brick buildings of the medical center. Leisure was theirs now and time to enjoy the world of nature; they had earned it. Almost every day, after a quiet breakfast, they walked to the conservation area just down the road from their suburban house. They crossed the small parking area and followed a trail that looped through the woods, around a pond, up over a low rise between meadows, and back again to the road and the beginning. They congratulated themselves that now, after years of work, of fitting home repairs and trimming the forsythia and mowing the lawn around the demands of their jobs, their choice of a semi-rural location was paying off. They would enjoy the changing seasons, the wayside flowers, the wild life, at last.

Over the years they had contributed money to the town's conservation effort. Walking, listening to the birds, chatting, bidding the occasional passerby good morning, they reaped the reward for their generosity. The well-maintained paths, the dredged pond that reflected the sky, the mowed meadow were all theirs to enjoy now. Beside the pond the town had placed a granite bench. During the first three years of their retirement, the couple walked briskly past the bench, savoring the odors of wet grass and mud from the margin of the pond in March or noting the thickening ice in December. The water sparkled blue in the sunshine, the reeds grew green and ripened into brown cattails, a red-winged blackbird flashed its colors to them.

In the fourth spring of their retirement, they still walked; they were determined to keep life normal, but now they stepped aside to let more vigorous walkers pass them and paused at the bench by the pond so the wife could rest. Although she tired quickly, she was making a good comeback, they assured each other. The scars from the surgery were healing. By the end of April she had gained a little weight. They did not remind each other as they sat side by side on the granite slab of the bench, their jackets shielding their thin haunches from the chilly stone, that in two weeks, when she was a little stronger, she would return to the city hospital for chemotherapy treatments.

All May and into June they walked, no matter what the weather. The treatments were not as debilitating as they had feared. Exercise would help her recovery; there were studies to prove it. She was determined to go out. Certainly, they believed, years of life in the suburbs, almost the country really, and their comfortable circumstances equipped them well to face nature. Their mudroom was well stocked with boots and coats and hats for all seasons. On a June morning, husband and wife, clad in light rain gear, sat on the bench as a fine drizzle puckered the surface of the pond. Young vegetation gleamed chartreuse and darker green, sunlight slanted pale gold through mist among the trees on the other side of the water. The couple sat silent. A bird somewhere to the right spilled an abrupt cadence of notes and then stopped as suddenly as it began. The reeds growing from the muck along the edge of the pond rustled.

"Oh look," the wife breathed.

A female mallard trailed by six ducklings paddled along the shallow edge of the pond. Puffs of yellow, they drifted on the water like pollen. They rode their mother's wake, gobbling at the fragments of green scum her passage scattered.

"How adorable," she said, and when the couple rose from the bench and walked on, she seemed to have more energy. She followed his pointing finger to see where the finches swooped up-and-down, up-and-down over the meadow, and noticed where the yellow flags were blooming again this year in the ditch beside the parking area.

The next morning was clear and bright. They walked at what seemed to the husband an almost normal pace. When she slowed, they sat on the bench by the pond. He took her hand in his. Her skin was thinner, more fragile, almost translucent across the back of her hand except for the blue-black bruise where the needle for the last treatment had been inserted. He did not mention that but held her hand lightly and talked of their children, grown now. Their daughter had called on her way to work this morning as she often did. She loved her job. Their son had met someone. He wanted to bring her to visit over the weekend.

"I am so glad," she said. "I plan to live to see my grandchildren."

The ducks came swimming from the other side of the pond.

"We should have brought some bread," she said and then, "but there are only five." She counted again. "Five."

"It could have been a fox," he said. He had heard that they were coming back to the area. He had heard reports of coyote, too. It could even have been a cat. They both knew that in a pond like this one there might be snapping turtles. Even a large fish could pull down a duckling, he supposed. Life is hard for small things.

"Yes," she said quietly.

She withdrew her hand from his and they walked on. The rise of the meadow smelled of blueberry.

"The bushes must be in bloom," he said. "We will have to remember to look for berries in a month or so."

They were due at the clinic early the next morning and did not take their walk. When they returned to their routine three days later, there were several mature ducks on the pond, eager to bob and quarrel over the crumbs of bread the couple strewed; but just three ducklings skittered across the pond behind the serene profile of the mother mallard. They scattered more bread and waited to see if laggard babies would emerge from the reeds. None came and the wife began to weep. She was just tired, she said. He blamed himself that he had pushed her to come out too soon. They rested a moment and then turned back to take the shortest route home.

The next day he insisted that they drive around to the other side of the conservation land. They could walk in the evergreen plantation there, where it smelled of peat and mushrooms on cool days or pungently of pine resin on hot ones. It was wiser because they were never far from the parking area there, he said. She could have the benefit of her walk without overtaxing herself. They did not mention the ducks.

Once or twice during the next month the husband walked the path to the pond by himself while his wife rested in the dimness of their blue-green and white bedroom, where the shades were drawn against the summer heat. While he sat on the granite bench and smoked the daily secret cigarette that he allowed himself, she dreamed of water running over rocks in a mountain stream. Just once, he saw the ducks again. The three survivors shepherded still by their dappled brown mother. They were larger now, their yellow fluff giving way to the brown of pinfeathers. They still gobbled eagerly at whatever floated on the water's surface or skittered off at a tangent and then came hurrying back to ride their mother's wake. One of them stretched its puny wings, flapping, trying to lift itself from the water.

In September, in a hospital in the heart of the city, the husband tiptoed into his wife's room and sat down beside her bed. He touched her hand lightly. Awakening from drugged sleep, she smiled at him.

"Are there six ducklings on the pond today?" she asked from the remote place where she lived now.

He was amazed that she remembered them.

"Yes," he lied, because what did it matter now. "They grow stronger every day. They practice flying. I imagine they will fly south very soon."

She lowered her veined eyelids over the round balls of her eyes and dreamed of birds resting on the still surface of a pond, feathered breast to mirrored breast. The pond she dreams is a bowl of silt and dark water. Curled brown oak leaves and yellow pollen float on the surface awhile and then sink. The pond's predators lie quiescent in the bottom mud, jaws clothed, teeth sheathed. She dreams of the great snapping turtle on whose back the world rests. She sees its wrinkled eyelids smooth themselves into hoods over the round balls of its ancient eyes. On the calm surface of the pond in the slanting rays of twilight, the brown and green and gold birds settle their plumage, tuck, first one and then another, their heads under their wings, and sleep.

Red Right Returning
Emily Moore

9 June, Sitka, Alaska

Coming back, diving in—Papa meets me at the Sitka airport and we drive to the *Medeia*, peer at the small orange submarine, the *Delta*, lashed to her deck. The *Delta* sits two people, dives to 1,200 feet on commission. Our dive will be comparatively shallow: a bounce dive, they call it, just a half hour's drop to ricochet off an underwater ledge. Still, we're the lucky ones; few guests are invited on this research sub, its dives reserved for the biologists who hire it. I'm glad to be onboard, gladder still to be back in Alaska.

Papa slips me a silver packet of Bonine, along with my mother's instructions to take one tablet an hour before leaving dock. It is a clear day by Southeast Alaskan standards—clouds high up and broken—but the wind is from the northeast and the water is already bumpy. In the wheelhouse, Wade, the *Medeia's* skipper, listens to the Coast Guard's weather advisory: winds to twenty-five knots.

"It'll be bouncy out there," he says. "Those of you who get seasick may want to lie low until it's your turn to dive."

I down the Bonine and stake out a place out on deck. The other guests along for the dive—Fish and Game biologists, a geologist from Montana—dump out their coffee and sip water instead. We turn our faces into the wind, fix our eyes on the sturdy slope of Mount Edgecumbe as the *Medeia* rolls out into Sitka Sound.

"You ready for this?" Mason, the first mate, asks me. He stands wide-legged in his Stormy Seas jacket, a coil of rope looped around the crook of his elbow. "You look a little woozy."

"I've been traveling," I say. "Too much. Just got in from Philly this morning."

Mason nods, commiserating. I point to his elbow and ask, "What's the rope for?"

He looks down at the coil, then back at me with a smile. "You mean the *line*? Come on, Emily, you grew up here and you don't know your lingo?"

I'd argue my case—I'm the black sheep in a family of fishermen—but just then the *Medea* lurches violently in a wave.

Mason grins at my green face. "The line's to steady the sub when we hoist her overboard," he says. "But it looks like we might need it to steady you. Lost your sea legs back east somewhere, did you?"

The dive itself: quiet, deep. I crouch on a foam cushion, peering through the portholes in the *Delta*'s sides. Dave, the pilot, sits on a stool behind me, looking out through the windowed hatch. The *Medeia*'s crane lowers us into the water and lets go; we bob away, open the ballasts to fill with water. We sink below the waves and switch the lights on, falling through ever darkening blues as Dave ticks off the depth to Wade through the surface communication system: 40 feet, 68 feet, 122 feet, roger that. I watch jellyfish rise past us like tiny ghosts, plankton disappear into the deep. But I'm more aware of weight than sight: my stomach settled, pressed after the churning on the surface; the back of my neck strangely weighted. When I touch my fingers to the window, I find it wet with condensation, as if the ocean is slowly seeping in.

We hit rock at 230 feet—*thunk!*—and Dave welcomes me to the bottom of the ocean. A strange world: lit by our spotlight and fragile laser beams, the place is barren, ghostly. Dave says the visibility is good—it's fifteen feet—but I see only rocks billowing with sediment and the red beads the laser beams string down their rigid threads. Then a mottled quillback rockfish darts from behind a rock, his sharp row of dorsal spines rising like the ruff of a wary cat. Nearby, there's a yelloweye—*Sebastes ruberrimus*—a juvenile, two white stripes running through the red of its body. And an adult yelloweye, maybe one foot long, comes to check us out, swimming beside my window as the *Delta* putts along.

"That fish is probably forty or fifty years old," Dave says. "We had no idea they were so old until recently, when people like your mom began to study them. I remember gillnetters finding them in their nets, tossing them overboard, thinking they weren't fully grown. Now we know how venerable they are. The *Delta* helps us study them in their own habitat, so hopefully we can learn a lot more."

I look at the gold disc of the rockfish's eye, which tilts up back and down again a foot outside my window. So little is known about this fish: how it nests, how it mates. The importance, then, of studying *in situ*, of observing the fish in the dark world it calls home. Habitat: "the place where one naturally lives and grows," the navigable place, where one can swim despite the murky waters. Perhaps humans are less dependent on their home place. I wonder how embedded I am in my own.

The half hour up, Dave alerts the *Medeia* that we're surfacing, and the *Delta* blasts the water from her tanks. We come up as if coming through dawn: the water taking on more light, illuminating a yellow haze of plankton. Then it breaks—we are sloshing at the surface, the windows bobbing between sea and sky, thick rivulets streaming down the glass on the upswing. The hatch twists open—my ears clear as Dave's feet push off the seat—and I'm pulled out onto the rolling boat, into the wind and sky.

10 June, Sitka
"The interior landscape responds to the character and subtlety of an exterior landscape," writes Barry Lopez: "The shape of the individual mind is affected by land as it is by genes." Standing on the *Medeia's* decks, watching as we approach the town of Sitka, I wonder how this landscape has shaped me—the broody skies, the quiet, the braided land and water. Already I feel calmer here, centered in a way I haven't been for what seems a very long while.

I've been traveling—this month in the traditional sense, but in another sense for the past six years. My time in two schools on the East Coast has been one of movement and change, a suspension, as in most travel, of place and of self to live in other worlds. I found myself facing new landscapes and peoples, new apartments and roommates, new ideas, new opinions, new loves. My sense of self shifted with every encounter. I know I'm young. My parents remind me constantly that I don't have to commit to any one path. But I've begun to feel ungrounded, unable to dig into any path at all—jobs, goals, a relationship of three years. I've come home for two months this summer before my last year in school, hoping to center myself by returning to a place I often long for.

But Alaska is not an easy home. Museums, restaurants, an influx of people and ideas—the things I have grown to love are not the mainstays of my state, a wilderness whose human population is barely half a million. I'm not a fisher or a hunter. I'd just as soon read a book as go outdoors. Yet I still respond deeply to this place, feel somehow embedded in it. Living elsewhere has always seemed temporary, an excursion away from the islands and quiet where I feel at home.

At school, I've been reading the literature of Alaska, hoping to find some guide for my own mixed feelings on the place. The titles are many: everything from Muir's travels to Michener's epic, John Haines's Interior to Barry Lopez's Arctic. John McPhee's portraits capture the burly side of the Alaska spirit; Richard Nelson paints a quieter kind, found in his communion with an island near his Sitka home. But in all of these pages, little has resonated with my own experience. Most books take place in latitudes farther north than my home in Southeast Alaska—a warmer, more watery place than the mainland's expansive cold. Many narratives are the product of escape: from the humdrum and the commodified, from a realm that has pushed aside the natural world. The writers of these books find healing in Alaska, or simply adventure; but once they find it, they leave. "A place made of imagination and ice," the essayist Brian Doyle writes, pronouncing Alaska "more a place to go than to be." Such lines reveal the state's mythic place in the cultural imagination, framing Alaska as a world apart, not a world to hunker down in. This doesn't speak to my childhood here. And it's not much help for finding a rooted place in these islands.

On shore in Sitka that night, staying with my father's old fishing friends, I lie in bed listening to Papa and Theo debate humanism and halibut quotas, thinking of them as people who have found their place here after a good deal of wandering. "When are you going to get out of school and figure out what you really want to do?" Theo had asked me at dinner, but I told him I didn't know. Outside, a stalk of fireweed sways beside the window, the light in the high overcast sky white and soft at 11:00 p.m.

15 June, Ketchikan
In Alaska's literature, Southeast gets short shrift. Lopez, Haines, McPhee—their narratives stay up north, McPhee nodding to the nubby arm of Southeast Alaska only to mention the capital. Sitka appears on a map on the inset of his book, which cannot be said for Ketchikan, my hometown, though it is Alaska's fourth largest city.

Southeast may not have the grandeur of the far north—not the ice or snow or months of darkness the word Alaska brings to mind—but it is a place of watery beauty. Flying over the labyrinth of waterways and islands to Ketchikan this morning, I think of Carolyn Servid, a Sitka author who found in Southeast the home she'd always wanted. "Rootedness in place," she writes, "provides an essential context and coherence that allows us to know who we are by way of where we are, that allows us to act, to move our lives into their own significance." She quotes the theologian Walter Brueggemann: "A sense of place is a primary category of faith." Looking at the islands and labyrinthine water beneath my window, I understand why Servid would choose to settle in Southeast. I, too, want to root myself in a ground I find holy.

It's raining, the usual for Ketchikan. I arrive on the morning flight from Sitka, and spend the afternoon visiting with my grandmother, my aunt Cheryl, and my uncle Hans in the green house beside the creek where my family has lived since the 1940s. They ask about school, about Tom ("We're taking a break," I tell them, and they nod quietly, Scandinavian to the core). Then they ask about my plans for after school.

"Actually, I've been thinking of coming back here," I say.

"Oh, no," Hans says immediately.

"To rainy old Southeast?" This is Cheryl. "What do you want to do—rot?" She chuckles, but her smile falls as she feeds the sewing machine a blanket she is making for her granddaughter. I know Cheryl wants to move south, to be closer to my cousin and the grandkids, not to mention to a little sun.

"I thought I'd teach," I say. "English at the high school or the junior high." I try to explain that I'd rather build a life around a place than follow a career willy-nilly. I want to be part of a community, I say, one whose lifestyle is shaped by the place that provides it.

"You can find that elsewhere," Hans insists. "This town is dying. You're forgetting winters—you haven't spent one here in a long time. Everything shuts down after the tourists leave."

"Everything," Cheryl says, and her needle stops mid-stitch. "Did you hear about the new ordinance the city passed this year—the one that keeps stores from being boarded up in the winter? The cruise ship companies still nail plywood to the inside of the windows, but at least they can't cover every storefront up with planks. Downtown used to be so eerie."

"So I won't come to Ketchikan," I hedge. "But Sitka or Juneau, maybe—they seem to have things going on."

"Southeast is all the same: wet and cold and miserable," Hans says. "You got out, you can make it out there. Don't mess that up by coming back."

I turn to my grandmother, hoping for a different response. She left her family in Minnesota for this town, worked to make Ketchikan a home. I know it wasn't always easy, but she's a fixture here, a community matriarch in local affairs.

But my grandmother folds her hands in her lap, reticent. "These are very small towns," she says.

16 June, Ketchikan
In Jonathan Raban's *Passage to Juneau*, Ketchikan is a friendly, redneck stop on the author's sail up the Inside Passage. Tying up to the harbor at Thomas Basin, Raban wanders the downtown, struck by the bikers he sees in the Pioneer Pantry and by the hoards of tourists in the streets. But Raban likes the town, the friendly locals and community events, and he imagines a cozy Ketchikan in winter: "In the dark and cold and rain, Ketchikan would be a warm and neighborly huddle on its rocky ledge, squeezed tight between the forest and the water . . . . For months on end, it would be like living aboard a ship at sea."

A ship at sea indeed. It's still raining, the town adrift between ocean and weeping sky. When I go out, I don full regalia: rain pants and raincoat, rubber boots and wool hat. I begin to remember what it is to live in a temperate rainforest. My raincoat smells moldy at the cuffs.

Despite the downpour, downtown Ketchikan is in the full frenzy of tourist season. Cruise ship passengers crowd the streets in plastic rain ponchos, stuffing cameras and curios into canvas bags. Jewelry stores have moved in with a vengeance: my bank displaced to a side street, the Fo'c'stle Bar—once a downtown institution—swallowed up by diamond displays and periwinkle trim. "How many can we take?" ran the paper's recent headline, but jewelry stores, apparently, sell even more than the Taiwanese totem shops. And there are plenty of buyers: today alone, Ketchikan hosts six ships—giant moving hotels that lumber up to dock, their prows painted with names like *Princess Dawn* and *Radiance of the Seas*. For six hours, the cruise ships unload more than nine thousand visitors into a town that houses thirteen thousand year round.

It's a frenzied day, but no one can blame the town for being pushy. With fishing and timber waning, Ketchikan's economy leans heavily on these three months of buyers. Even the loggers have turned to tourists, revving their chainsaws and scaling logs in a timber show for crowds at an outdoor arena. I spot a specimen of another dying breed—a fisherman—making his way through the crowd of shoppers. In the sea of canvas bags and cameras, he looks entirely out of place.

I duck into a harbor to escape the crowds and run into a childhood friend, now a fisherman himself. Burt is two years younger than me, but at twenty-two he knows what he wants and has bought his first commercial fishing boat. The *Spawn* is a wooden troller in need of major work, Burt tells me. "It's going to be tricky with prices as low as they are this summer," he says. "But I'll make it somehow."

I listen to Burt's calculations of fuel and permit costs, find myself praying he can make it. The onslaught of farmed Chilean and Norwegian salmon plunged the price for wild Alaska fish, and many of the older fishermen have put their boats and permits up for sale. But here is Burt: young, gung-ho, determined. He's worked his way up to skipper, crewing on a number of boats, using his college money to attend a shipwright school. He has the knowledge needed to pull a living from this water, a knowledge I don't have, despite growing up in a family that did. Burt has a place here. I want him to be able to keep it.

"Come for a ride on The *Spawn* sometime," Burt says, giving me a hug in parting. "You'll see how good she sits in the water."

I laugh, wondering what else a boat could do.

"You'd be surprised. Some boats ride better than others. This one feels right at home."

22 June, Ketchikan

The distinction between local and outsider: a big deal where place lends identity. On Deer Mountain this morning, trying to work out my funk through vigorous hiking, I meet a couple from England who are amazed to learn I grew up here. "You live here?" they ask. "Well, lived," I say, and that seems to make more sense. They ask about winters, about school and the change of going away. When they wonder if I miss Alaska, I tell them that I'm thinking of coming back. But my center is shaken, my doubts rising.

Tonight at the Chinese restaurant, my stepfather, Neal, hears my thoughts of coming back and reacts: "Oh, don't just retreat back here." As if my return means defeat, a slinking back from an encounter with the world out there. I flinch. I don't want my parents adding to my own doubts. They've been in town for a week, taking time off from their jobs in Juneau to be with me in the house. But it is not a perfect reunion; their questions as to where I'm going and what I want rub harsh on what I don't know myself. My reticence may be juvenile, but I want to carve my own place here, on my own terms. I try to argue against us both.

"I see it as a choice," I say to Neal. "Something positive. It's not like Alaska is default."

"Then I question your choice," Neal counters, reminding me of the sagging economy, the weather, the turn to conservative politics in the state.

My mother puts down her ginseng tea. "Don't you want to go somewhere new?" she asks. "A city maybe—DC and all those free museums? You're young, Emily, you can always come back to Alaska later."

"But I'm tired of flitting around to different places," I insist. "Especially when they're not places where I'd want to stay. I want to start building something somewhere I could see myself long-term."

"But how do you know you can't build somewhere else if you don't give it a chance?" my mother asks. She picks up her chopsticks, pauses. "And if you're not bringing Tom—well, Emily, who will you actually meet here?"

I feel overwhelmed, nothing but a private hope to answer my parents' doubts.

I go to the bar that night, wanting to get out of the house. My friend Karta meets me at the Sourdough, bearing news of her impending marriage to a man she met in Spokane, a place they'll gladly leave for Alaska.

"You'd think I'd be the last one to come back," Karta muses, sipping her rum and Coke. "Remember how much I hated it here in high school? But it's different when you've been gone awhile. I want to be in a town again, a town with a strong community."

I eye her, suspicious of this 180 from her violent complaints in school. It's been six years since we left, and I wonder if both of us have made Ketchikan into a lost and sacred home, a place that's perfect only in our longing. I want to probe her reasons for some fault in my own, but just then a girl we knew from last summer—an East Coast kayak guide named Laura—spots us and slides into our booth. We swap updates, and I mention that I'm thinking of moving back.

"Are you single?" Laura asks, looking at both of us. Karta wags her finger with its ring.

I shrug. "I don't know. I'm not sure that he'd want to come here."

"Well," Laura says, sitting back in her booth, "this is a rotten place for singles. I've been working here for a year now and there's nobody. It's brain drain in the winter here—everyone our age who is interesting goes away."

As if on cue, a man we knew in high school saunters over to our booth. Jim leans against our table, one hand on his Miller Light, speaking vaguely of "the system." He tells us he came back after college ("the system hasn't gotten hold of Alaska yet") and has spent much of his time since drunk. He leans closer, his breath hot on my face. "Can't say I'm proud of it, though. Like quicksand around here—pulls you in and you're stuck. Except this is K-town, so it's more like a mud hole, or a muskeg—no, a shit hole! That's it—a shit hole!" He throws back his head and laughs.

Laura leans across the table when he leaves. "See what I mean?" she whispers. "All the interesting ones go away." She shakes her head, looks hard at us.

"If I had grown up in a town like this," she says, "I'd never come back."

22 June, Ketchikan
"I undertook this work not as a travel guide but as a guide to nontravel. My hope is to acclaim the rewards of exploring the place in which a person lives rather than searching afar, of becoming fully involved with the near-at-hand, of nurturing a deeper and more committed relationship with home." Walking downtown this morning, I think of Richard Nelson's commitment to Southeast Alaska, his desire to root here and grow. Why can't I find anyone in Ketchikan who feels the same way?

I pick my way among the tourists on Creek Street, thinking of what it means to be Alaskan. How can one claim an identity so obscured in myth? Native Alaskans have been pushed aside for the rugged individualist of Alaskan lore, the travel brochures and bestsellers touting the frontier life. The titles themselves are revealing: Peter Jenkins' *Looking for Alaska,* McPhee's *Coming into the Country,* anthologies like

The Last New Land. Alaska, they suggest, is a *tabula rasa*, a frontier not yet inscribed by the grid of the Lower Forty-eight. Adventure is still possible here, self-definition the norm. While there is some truth to these ideas, I find the literature on them overwrought. The insistence on Alaska as a frontier seems more the creation of a culture trapped by its own pressures than it does a reflection of Alaska's everyday.

In Miss Lillian's Parnassus Bookstore, the oldest on Creek Street, I find a title that resonates: *Our Alaska: Personal Stories about Life in the North*. The book's editor, an Anchorage journalist, published the stories to "redress the imbalance between the Alaska imagined by people who don't live here, and the Alaska we live in every day." But even as the stories emphasize the berry picking, the artist's studio, the office job paired with subsistence hunting, the book's urban Alaska authors win out over Native Alaskans and narrators in the bush. I wonder whose Alaska "our Alaska" can ever be, who gets to define which "outsiders" mis-imagine "us." Walking home that day, I question my own definitions: what stories have I turned to to claim Alaska mine?

28 June, Prince of Wales Island

The Turbo Otter is quieter than the Beavers I knew as a child. I ride shotgun beside the pilot, watching Ketchikan disappear behind the hump of Gravina Island. We are flying west, crossing the gray expanse of Clarence Straits, when the pilot lets me take the yoke.

"Three axes," he says into the headset's microphone, showing me the levers that tilt us right and left, forward and backward, and the foot pedal that drops the plane out from under our stomachs. I wag the wings a little, tipping the plane like the brim of a hat, but when the mountains of Prince of Wales Island loom before us, I hand the flying back to John. These little planes have never been my favorite—every year a few go down, victim to wind and fog—but they're essential transportation in Southeast, where most of the runways are water.

The shoreline of Prince of Wales—POW, as the locals call it—stretches as far as I can see. After Kodiak and Hawaii, it's the third largest island in the US. The pilot will drop me off in Craig, the island's biggest town (population two thousand), where my papa will pick me up. We're spending the weekend in Naukati, a former logging camp on the west coast of POW, where Papa has three acres and the rudiments of an A-frame cabin. We've come here once a year since I was eight; the island has already changed, its rugged logging camps disappearing or settling into towns.

Papa meets me at the plane dock and we get in his rental truck, surprisingly nice compared to the rickety ones we've had in the past. Our drive will take us north on gravel roads, the former logging routes that make Prince of Wales home to the most extensive road system in Southeast Alaska. Here you can actually cruise for an hour or more, crank up a tape in the deck and talk as the scenery rolls by. Papa plays Count Basie as we drive past Big Salt Lake and the turnoff to El Capitan caves, where an entire football stadium—bleachers and all—could fit into one of the caverns. Above ground, our view is a mosaic of clear cuts: mountains carved up into pieces, corridors of trees left like strips of green ribbon on a barren calico. Much of the island is patterned this way, Prince of Wales having supplied a good deal of timber for Ketchikan's former pulp mill.

My father is angry when he sees a new clear cut on Forest Service land, a hillside of slash that reaches clear to the road. "Remember the stretch of trees here?" he asks as we drive past a field of stumps. "Some of the last old growth cedars on this road. Damn it, they should have kept those at least—people need to see how big those trees get." I remember them: giant sentinels looming beside the road. Their absence strikes me, the stumps a haggard vestige of what once was. I think of Richard Nelson's description of a clear cut near his home in Sitka: "A gathering of ancients once stood here. Now it reminds me of a prairie in the last century, strewn with the bleached bones of buffalo."

And yet I'm wary of condemning logging altogether. What is the fate of these Southeast communities if they are denied a year-round economy? My father and I argue about this. Tourism hasn't yet come to Prince of Wales—and what, I ask, is the future in a three-month industry dominated by Caribbean corporations? The region has precious little economic diversity. I was a senior in high school when the Ketchikan pulp mill closed, when the town lost several hundred jobs and many of my friends moved away. Naukati, too, has struggled: just this year the logging camp closed, forcing residents to move to Coffman Cove or turn to whatever small jobs they could find. I want this region to survive, not just as a tourist attraction, but as a place where people and trees can thrive.

"Maybe so," Papa says, "but they could have kept those cedars." We rattle past the great gash in the mountain, trying to look ahead.

In Naukati, Papa and I spend the afternoon burning brush from the lower section of his lot, where second-growth hemlock once grew so densely even deer detoured the area. Papa had hired his neighbor to clear it, and the slash from his thinning is thick. I tug at stumps and branches, throwing them on one of three bonfires we built on the lot. The ground beneath the slash is brown and wet—nothing had been able to grow here. This is the aftermath of logging, too: trees jockeying for light, growing up dense and skinny instead of grand. I pull angrily at the slash, my back aching, my eyes prickling from the smoke.

We work through the afternoon, rain drizzling occasionally, sun breaking through the clouds at other times. By dinner, I am exhausted. I ease myself onto a wide stump, stare up at the ash drifting in the sunlight that has just pierced the needles of a spruce tree. It is a good tired, I realize: a feeling of having worked, of having done something with my hands and back. I think of John Haines' line from *The Stars, The Snow, The Fire:* "It is the plain life: the air, the cold, the hard work; and having eaten, the body rests and the mind turns to sleep." I know this life draws many people to Alaska. And yet I admit to myself that it isn't a lifestyle I often choose: my head takes the lead, my body, for the most part, simply tagging along behind.

Lying in my sleeping bag that night, listening to the patter of raindrops on the A-frame's blue tarp roof, I ask my father how he knew he'd found his place. Papa was twenty-four when he came from Oregon to Southeast Alaska; he told me once he knew the minute he stepped off the ferry that these islands would be home. "But it took a lot of wandering before I found it," he tells me now, rolling over in his sleeping bag to go to sleep. "Don't worry about your place yet, Emily. Let it find you."

4 July, Juneau
Fifty-five degrees in downtown Juneau. Standing near the Goldbelt Hotel, waiting for the parade to start, Neal grumbles: "The Fourth of July is supposed to be hot." My mother fluffs his hair, tells him to be thankful it's not raining. And she has a point: last night the firework show was cancelled, the clouds so low they would have drowned out

the lights. This morning the skies are lifting, giant mountains emerging black and soaring above the town. It's a chilly backdrop for the Fourth, perhaps, but certainly a stunning one.

My parents and I are getting along this time, having called a truce on the discussions of the future. All week the weather was stunning, and my mother and I hiked to take advantage of the sun: Monday to Granite Basin, Tuesday to the end of the Perseverance Trail. Wednesday we were crossing the muskegs of Mount Jumbo when a porcupine and her baby came padding up the boardwalk—pigeon-toed, grunting like tiny pigs. We stepped to the side; they passed us nonplussed, baby waddling under mother's spiny tail.

This afternoon, the clouds lifting fully to open skies, I will hike Mount Juneau by myself. My mother can't break away from a Fish and Game picnic, and she wasn't up for the trail anyway—"the steepest I ever saw," according to a hiker we met in Granite Basin. But I'm going, inspired by John Muir's *Travels In Alaska*, his account of scaling peaks with nothing but a compass and a biscuit in his pocket. Maybe I'm falling for the romanticism of Alaska's outdoorsmen after all.

I pack more than a biscuit—a PB-and-J, an apple, cheese, and water—and bring my father's copy of *Trees and Shrubs of Southeast Alaska*. I want to know my flora, taken as I am by Muir's ability to read the land. (His language, though a tad frilly to my modern ear, moves me with its rapture: "the wondrous beauty of the psalm-singing, lichen-painted trees," "the outcry of a newborn berg.") Peering at flowers along the trail, I try to match them to pictures in my father's book: river beauties, foam flower, Sitka rose. The deeply riveted bark of black cottonwoods is new to me; I learn from reading that this is the first tree to root in the moraine. In Ketchikan the glaciers left much earlier, the cottonwoods having ceded to spruce and cedar trees, the edges of ice-gnawed rock rubbed down by wind and rain.

Ensconced in flowers, loitering near the start of the trail, I am startled by three joggers returning from their run. "Not sure how far you're going," one says, panting, "but there's a bear up past Granite Creek. We think she has cubs, too—she charged our dog."

I thank them for the heads up. My turnoff to Mount Juneau comes long before Granite Creek, but I decide to put my book away, keep my eyes and ears open and get going on the trail.

The trail up Juneau switches back and forth across the mountain, alternating between open salmonberry thickets and narrow swathes of spruce trees. I'm at subalpine level by the time I take the turnoff; the few trees that grow here are stunted, twisted by wind. When I stop for swigs of water, I look back into Silverbow Basin, cupped between the massive peaks of Mount Juneau and Mount Roberts. Far below, downtown is a mosaic of buildings glinting in the sun. But the peak still looms above me.

It's hot. I realize I have forgotten a hat, so unaccustomed am I to preparing for sun. I splash water on my face and start up the trail again, which turns into a rocky creek bed rising vertically up the mountain. Later, I'll realize this was my mistake. A missed right off the creek bed, one faded strip of orange tape marking the exit through the bushes. A tricky turnoff, and a steep trail afterward—but a trail with ropes, steps hacked out of the rock. I have bypassed this, charged straight up the creek bed, thinking I know my way.

At some point it gets bad. I'm clawing my way through salmonberry bushes, pulling myself up the slope. I have a hard time finding footing; the trail is growing fainter, its angle up the mountain impossibly steep. "Is this really a public trail?" I keep asking myself, and finally shout it out loud at the mountain. But I've convinced myself this is the way, and once I cross a narrow precipice—edging one heel across its ledge, digging my fingers so hard into the rock my skin will bear the imprint for a day—there is no turning back.

My father will tell me later that people die every year on this mountain, victim to its slopes and narrow trails. Already an eighteen-year-old boy was lost this summer, his body found in a ravine after his parents missed him in line to board their cruise ship. I am lucky. I arrive at the windswept peak two hours after my turnoff from the creek bed, having survived another scare of tumbling rocks and scrub-branch hand-holds. I sink onto the mountaintop, stunned by both the view and the adrenaline. 360 degrees of ocean, mountain, and emerald islands spread before me: Stephen's Passage on the backside of Douglas Island, Mansfield Peninsula, and the white-peaked Chilkat Range. Below, eagles swoop above the sparkling channel, Juneau a toy town along its shore. I turn to the mountains behind me, follow their craggy ridges to the ice field they shoulder, spot the green valley of Silverbow Basin far below. (I also see—most glorious—the trail, flagged and roped; the sight makes me weak with relief.) The view is incredible, a beauty that would send Muir into ecstasy. And there is a part of me that responds deeply to this place, to the expanse of mountains, sea, and sky that awed me even as a child.

But another part of me feels sick, woozy. I am verging on sun stroke, weakened by the surge of adrenaline. I lie down flat between clumps of purple lupine, throw an arm across my eyes and wait for the world to stop spinning.

10 July, Juneau
In his journal of 1879, Jon Muir wrote: "I have found southeastern Alaska a good, healthy country to live in. The climate of the islands and shores of the mainland is remarkably bland and temperate and free from extremes of either heat or cold throughout the year. It is rainy, however—so much so that haymaking will hardly ever be extensively engaged in here, whatever the future may show in the way of the development of mines, forests, and fisheries. This rainy weather, however, is of good quality, the best of the kind I ever experienced, mild in temperature, mostly gentle in its fall, filling the fountains of the rivers and keeping the whole land fresh and fruitful."

Last day for me in Juneau. For dinner, Papa and I walk to the Fiddlehead Café, where we will order my favorite ginger halibut stir-fry. But the walk is tasty, too: we make hors d'oeuvres of the blueberries, huckleberries, and juicy salmonberries that grow along the way. I think of Muir's "fruitful" land, how apt his description remains despite the dearth of hay.

At the Fiddlehead, we run into Chandra, a former Ketchikanite I knew in school. Chandra is a mother now, her partner a Baltimore man who loves her Alaska home. Talking with Chandra, her daughter peeking over her shoulder from the backpack where she sits, I am moved by the image they present: mother and child, curls lit golden from the low sun of the window. They are beautiful, young, placed somehow, together here and building a life.

But Chandra interrupts my reverie. "We're doing okay for being stuck here," she says, half smiling, half not. "Sean has a job he loves; mine is okay. There're good people here, good hikes and all. But there's so much I'd like Nova to try that isn't available in Southeast."

She adjusts the backpack, Nova's head bobbing in the light. "Don't fool yourself, Emily," Chandra says. "Don't forget that these are really small towns."

19 July, Ketchikan
Back in Ketchikan again, gearing up for the last leg of this trip home. I've signed up for my first commercial fishing experience, working as the cook on my uncle Hans's boat. The day before we leave, I bake lasagna, seal salad in a Tupperware bowl. The state permit I need as a crew member costs me $60, half the price non-residents pay. At the local tackle shop, I stand in line with three burly men from Seattle, whose worn Helly Hansens and fishing talk attest to their experience. They seem surprised when I request a fishing permit, a female dressed in khakis and leather sandals. I like their shock. I pay my $60 when they pay $120, feeling smug to be a "certified" Alaskan.

That evening, my grandmother asks if I'd like to learn to make bread. How does she know these things—that I want to learn to make something of sustenance? We feed the yeast some sugar, mix with flour, and begin to knead. Waiting for the dough to rise, my grandmother asks for eight stalks of rhubarb to make a pie. I pull on my rain gear, go to the garden and flick the slugs off the red stalks. I twist the stalks off as she has taught me: close to the base, leaving two stalks to every plant. Once, my grandmother told me, she picked rhubarb all the way till Labor Day, and the next summer the plants were paltry, thin. To know these things: to stay in place for several seasons, to learn the ways of plants like your very body. How else to know your rhubarb but to pluck it every year?

As I come inside, the rain begins to downpour. I hand my grandmother the rhubarb stalks as I wrestle off my rain gear, ask if she ever wanted to leave Ketchikan and go back to Midwestern summers. "I thought about it sometimes," she says, rinsing the rhubarb off in the sink. "But this was home, and that was that." She brings the rhubarb to the table, begins to cut the stalks into one-inch cubes before pausing to listen to the rain, which is pounding now like veritable Minnesota dairy cattle on the roof. "Can you believe it, I actually missed this weather when I'd visit Glencoe," she says. "I wanted to stand on the dock, let the storms wash over me," she laughs, looking up at her imagined tempest, holding the rhubarb out across the dinner table like she's receiving grace.

20 July, Ketchikan
At 7:00 a.m., I meet Hans at the bottom of the hill and we walk to the harbor. He briefs me on the stats: pink salmon are seven cents a pound, up one cent from last year; sockeye, at sixty-five cents, are what we hope to get. We have three days to fish—the gill net openings run Sunday through Thursday, but Hans must return early to work at the Harbormaster ("the job that pays," he says). "And if this weather doesn't improve, we may not even fish today," Hans adds. "They're warning twenty-knot winds, so we'll just see how far we get down the channel. It ain't worth getting excited about one missed day when fish are seven cents a pound."

We leave the harbor at 7:20, nosing out the narrow opening between the jetty and the tour ship *Princess Dawn*. The channel is rough; it's worse once we leave the protection of Pennock Island. The *Kyrion* lurches across the whitecaps, and, for the umpteenth time this summer, my stomach lurches, too. I lie down flat on the bunk in the galley, trying not to mind the rolling waves.

By ten, Hans has glanced at my green face and decided not to rough it. We duck into a cove at Annette Island, and Hans goes below for a nap. I stay awake, not realizing a nap would help me later; I read and stand on deck. It's quiet here, the cove fringed in fog and cedar trees. Looking at the beach I'd like to explore, I realize suddenly that I will not leave this boat for several days. Instantly I feel claustrophobic, struck by the ironies that have marked my entire summer: this feeling out-of-place even as I seek to ground myself in place, claustrophobic on a boat on open water, motion sick at every turn. I stand at the edge of the *Kyrion*'s bow, wishing I had the option, at least, of stepping off the boat to walk away.

Hans is up at 2:00 a.m., scratching his head, lighting the stove, scanning the water in the gray light I cannot tell from dusk or dawn. We made a run last night when the weather lulled, anchoring up at Cat Island farther down the channel, but it's still three hours to the fishing grounds at Tree Point. I sit up when the engine roars, wanting to be awake, but when the boat starts to bounce again, I sink back into my sleeping bag. I am lucky that Hans is not a "screecher," an infamous species of skipper who would resent my truancy on the bunk. Hans is taciturn, quietly solicitous. He tells me to go back to sleep.

It's 4:00 a.m. when I wake to the slowing of the engine. Full daylight now, though filtered by a heavy overcast. Through the port-side windows, I glimpse the craggy coast of Tree Point, surf breaking against its cliffs.

Hans is pulling on his rain gear. "Time to fish?" I ask, trying to sound eager and awake. Hans calls "yep" from the door.

The floor is not where it was when I looked to land on it. Instantly, I feel sick. I stumble to the head, sit on the miniature seat trying to stabilize myself against the walls. The cord to the overhead light swings violently, tapping me alongside my ear. I don my raingear in the galley, clamber out on deck to gasp the salty air.

Hans is checking the drum when I find him; he steps aside to let me pass. "You feel okay?" he asks.

"I don't know. I think I'm better now."

"Just take it easy," Hans says, pulling on his gloves. "There's no need to get sick over fish."

He presses the foot pedal and the heavy drum on the *Kyrion*'s stern pulls in the net, wrapping the green mesh around its middle. Our first fish is a pink salmon, its white belly crimped in mesh. Hans shows me how to "pick" the fish, freeing its gills and body from the net with a small metal hook. It takes a good half-minute before the fish is untangled and sent down a chute to the ice hatch.

"A lot of trouble for forty-two cents," Hans mutters.

I try my hand at the next fish—a chum salmon this time, eight pounds at twenty cents each, and still alive—but I can't find the top or bottom of the net, and my efforts to do so only entangle the fish more. Meanwhile, the *Kyrion* is lurching to and fro, and the wriggling fish and confusion of nets make my stomach churn.

Hans catches sight of my face. "Watch the shore line—something steady," he says, but it's too late: the plum I ate this morning comes straight up and splatters overboard. I lean over the side until I can stand up, feeling weak but not as queasy. The smell of plum lingers in my nose.

Hans looks at me. "You okay?"

I nod, but the boat lurches again, and I swallow hard against my stomach.

"Why don't you go lie down," Hans suggests. "You'll get your sea legs after a while, but until then there's no need to be miserable."

I lie down on my bunk. I will spend my first day fishing here.

When Jonathan Raban passed Tree Point in his sailboat in the late 1990s, he was struck by "the daunting armada" of the gill net boats: "The entrance to Revillagigedo Channel, nearly ten miles across, was blocked solid with small boats. From where I was, it looked as if a swarm of bugs had settled on the water, like blowflies on a carcass."

Unflattering similes aside, Raban's description strikes me for the sheer contrast in numbers. Our first day at Tree Point, I spot four, maybe five boats, including the yellow *Spraycatcher* that keeps running close to our corks. Hans guesses several skippers have gone up north, where hatchery fish promise a steady stream of chum salmon; but many, he says, just aren't fishing. The *Ketchikan Daily News* reported recently that two hundred seine boats are fishing this summer, about half the long-term average. Prices are so bad, the article said, a hold of fish barely pays the fuel bill; many skippers keep their boats tied up to dock.

From my bunk in the galley, where I lie flat all of Monday trying to control my stomach, I can see the *Spraycatcher* reel in its nets. A few other boats announce their presence on the VHF radio, chiming in on channel 16 with the mantra of boat talk: "*Betty Jean, Betty Jean,* this is the *Loki,* over." "Copy *Loki,* this is *Betty Jean,* meet you on channel 6, over." Channel 16 is the hailing frequency, and the Coast Guard monitors it for emergencies. I hear one Mayday that afternoon—"Shouldn't we try to help?" I shout to Hans, having stumbled onto deck like the green-horn that I am—but the Canadian Coast Guard reports a rescue soon after, much sooner than the three hours it would have taken us to reach the site. I sink onto my bunk, relieved for the boat, wishing something would rescue my Maydayed guts.

Tuesday morning, my sea legs have miraculously appeared. The quiet anchorage of our night at Fire Island brought my appetite back; I ate lasagna out on deck, watching the sky glow red behind the island's dark silhouette. Sitting there, listening to the crash of surf on the island's outer edge and to the call of a Swainson's thrush from the shoreline trees, I began to sense the beauty my father always found in fishing: the long days that made for welcome rest, an evening's anchorage near islands one would otherwise never see.

We head out at 3:00 a.m., pick our first set at 6:00. The day promises good weather, though Dixon Entrance, at the mouth of the Pacific Ocean, always has a swell. I am relieved when the waves don't bother me, and I set to work, hoping to make up for the previous day. But it turns out I'm no good at picking, either; I struggle to free one fish while Hans has finished three.

"That's all right," Hans says, throwing his fish down the ice hatch. "We don't want you to like fishing."

But my uncle is happy with the weather, I can tell, and that I'm feeling better. Plus we're catching sockeye, the "always welcome" fish at sixty-five cents a pound. We pick the nets, counting the catch in Hans's terms: two always welcome, three never welcome (pinks). Chum and coho are kind of welcome. The stray steelhead goes in a basket for dinner when we get home.

When Hans starts another set and goes below for a nap, I watch the cork line, making sure the boat doesn't get tangled in the net. This, at least, is one task I *can* do. Between checks, I try to read the GPS charts on Hans's laptop computer. My uncle has joined the ranks of wireless fishermen who position themselves on screen: a cryptic chart of numbers, fathoms, buoys. I want to know his language. When we passed a red buoy in the channel, my uncle kept it port side, while the boat coming toward us, bound for harbors home, kept the buoy on its right. "Red right returning," my uncle explained, and I worked hard to remember the mnemonic's rules. Such shorthand for the right of way, such buoys and maps that chart a way out and back again—don't they speak to our need to position ourselves, to fix our place even when we are *en route*? We want to know how far we have come and how long until we get where we are going. We use the markers—the red, the right—to find a return route home.

My uncle and I haul our last set at 8:00 p.m., fire up the engine for the run to Foggy Bay. We'll unload our catch to a tender there, tally up the weight and take the check: $1,200 for three days' work. Hans seems satisfied, but to me he says, "I hope this has wiped any idea from your head of wanting to be a fisherman." I tell him not to worry.

I'm tired. On the ride to Foggy Bay, I fall asleep on my bunk, the surging waves only rocking me to sleep. I dream of the walks I'll take when I'm on shore again: around Ward Lake, up and down Park Avenue, all along the solid streets of town.

I'm awakened when Hans shouts through the doorway. "Emmy, come here! I want you to smell this." I climb out on deck: a fragrant warmth greets my face, surprising after the smack of sea air. It's a mix of muskeg and cedar, fungi and sweet-smelling spice. Turning to look at Hans, I see him standing at the helm, the wind beating the cords of his rain jacket against his face.

"Land!" he shouts, and he is smiling.

30 July, Ketchikan
"How many of us have the luxury of returning to the landscape we inhabited as children?" Franklin Burroughs asks, quoting Wordsworth's belief that in our childhood home we find the "language of our former hearts." Traveling in Ireland a few summers ago, my friend Mandy and I came across a local talent show in a school gymnasium. Out on that lacquered, dimly lit floor, beribboned children performed Irish step dancing, wobbling on their ankles in ways I thought would make them break. A small boy brought a penny whistle to the mic and peeped out a jig; an old couple danced on the sidelines. Near the end of the night, the emcee called up a man from the audience to tell an Irish tale. At first, the man refused to go, shaking his head and smiling, but eventually the audience prodded him to talk. They knew the stories, and what was more, they knew who among them could tell the stories best. I remember watching as everyone in that gymnasium listened rapt to the man's tale—the way the smallest child sensed a story was being told, a story that explained why she was there and what she was meant to do. Maybe we have to be wary of such stories, of the limits and roles they enforce, but we can't deny our desire for a few. Sitting in that gymnasium, I wanted so much to belong to that kind of community: to share the stories of a place, to understand my relationship with the people and the culture that grew in a specific corner of the earth.

As my days wane in Alaska, I go for one more trip beneath the waves. Brooke, a high school friend who lives on a sailboat with her husband and two friendly dogs, has invited me to snorkel off her boat. I drive to the cove where her family has a dock; we wrestle on our wet suits. It's a beautiful day, the sun high and clear and the blue water of the channel sparkling. We dive in from the stern of Brooke's sailboat, make our way along the underwater shore: golden fronds of seaweed swaying in the waves, hermit crabs retracting into their shells when our shadows fall across them. When touched, brilliant pollups of red sea snails disappear into their white tube shell. We spot some fish—Brooke can name them—and note where the shelf drops off into the deeper channel. The light filters through the waves as a grid of rippling hexagons, patterning the ocean floor like an underwater beehive. Our breathing is rhythmic, meditative: drawing in a breath through the snorkel tube, releasing it to the sky. Brooke points to a school of smolt, and they dart like a hundred shards of light away from her finger.

Goggle-eyed underwater, I am amazed to realize that I lived eighteen years on this ocean's edge: always on the surface. Like my dive in the *Delta* at the beginning of the summer, seeing beneath the waves stuns me, to realize the other worlds out there, the adaptation of things to their specific nook. The more I look, the more I realize how little I know of home.

31 July, Ketchikan
Last day: a frenzy of packing, goodbyes to friends, a run along Ward Lake where a fly fisherman's line catches the light: a golden thread snaking against the trees.

For dinner, I go to the Freitags; long-time family friends whose children I have watched grow up. Mari and Jess take me to the net fort at the back of their house: twenty-one seine nets strung up in tiers in the trees. We bound from one level to the next, jumping off one layer only to be caught by another, landing, finally, in a hammock-like net to talk. Jess tells me about graduating from high school and his plans to attend college in Oregon. "I can't wait to get out of Ketchikan," he says. I tell him I used to feel the same way.

At home, I check my ticket, scan the bookshelf for a companion on the long flight back east. Something not Alaskan; it's time to transition into a different world. I settle on Ha Jin's *Waiting*, stuff it in my backpack with Raban's *Passage to Juneau*. In case, I tell myself, and zip the bags shut so they'll be ready.

Before I go to bed, I stand awhile at the front door, looking out the three diagonally spaced windows and listening to the creek rush its way to the falls. I picture the salmon there, pushing their way home after three or four or even seven years in the ocean. How they find their way back here—to that one birthing stream among thousands that empty into the ocean—this is still a mystery, a homing instinct scientists cannot explain.

I wonder about my own instincts. I know there is time for other places, time to come back later, if I should choose. I would like to be at home wherever I am, finding a place and a community of my own making. But standing at the door, listening to the creek and watching the alder trees wave in the streetlight as I have every year of my life, I doubt I'll shake my longing for this place. I'll always be coming back.

notes on contributors

DAN ALBERGOTTI'S poems have appeared in *Ascent, Meridian, Mid-American Review, New Orleans Review, Prairie Schooner, The Virginia Quarterly Review*, and other journals. He was a Tennessee Williams Scholar at the 2003 Sewanee Writers' Conference, a fellow at the Virginia Center for the Creative Arts in July 2004, and the Richard Soref Scholar in Poetry at the 2004 Bread Loaf Writers' Conference. His chapbook, *Charon's Manifest*, won the 2005 Randall Jarrell/Harperprints Chapbook Competition, and one of his poems was reprinted in *Best New Poets 2005*. He is also the winner of the 2005 Oneiros Press Poetry Broadside Competition. A graduate of the MFA program at the University of North Carolina Greensboro and former poetry editor of *The Greensboro Review*, he currently serves as poetry editor of *storySouth* (www.storysouth.com) and teaches at Coastal Carolina University.

KAREN E. BENDER is the author of the novel *Like Normal People* (Houghton Mifflin, 2000) and co-editor of the forthcoming anthology *Choice* (MacAdam/Cage). Her fiction has appeared in *The New Yorker, Zoetrope: All-Story, Best American Short Stories, Best American Mystery Stories*, and the *Pushcart Prize* series.

JONATHA CEELY was born in Kingston, Ontario. She has lived in Turkey and Italy, and currently lives and works in Brookline, Massachusetts. Her first novel, *Mina*, was published in 2004 by Delacorte Press, and her second, *Bread and Dreams*, by Delacorte Press in 2005. She is presently working on her third novel, set primarily in Ontario and Massachusetts in contemporary times.

CHRISTOPHER COKINOS is at work on a nonfiction book for Tarcher/Penguin tentatively titled *The Fallen Sky: A Private History of Shooting Stars*. The winner of a Whiting Writers' Award, Cokinos is the founding editor of *Isotope* and has work forthcoming in *Orion* and *Turnrow*. He has appointments in English and Natural Resources at Utah State University.

ELIZABETH CRANE is the author of two previous story collections, *When the Messenger is Hot* (Little, Brown, 2003) and *All This Heavenly Glory* (Little, Brown, 2005). Her work has also been featured in publications including *Other Voices, Nerve*, the *Chicago Reader*, and the *Believer*, as well as several anthologies, including *McSweeney's Future Dictionary of America, The Best Underground Fiction, The Best Show of Their Lives, Loser, After*, and *Altared*. She is the author of the blog Standby Bert (www.elizabethcrane.com/blog/index.html), read by at least a dozen people on a regular basis. Crane is also a regular contributor to *Writer's Block Party* on WBEZ Chicago, a columnist for *Punk Planet*, and two of her short stories have been featured on NPR's *Selected Shorts*. In October 2003, she received the Chicago Public Library Twenty-first Century Award, granted by the Chicago Public Library Foundation. Crane teaches creative writing at Northwestern University's School of Continuing Studies, the School of the Art Institute, and the University of Chicago. She lives in Chicago with her husband, Ben, and their dog, Percy.

TENAYA DARLINGTON has worked as a knife seller, an X-ray librarian, a back-up singer for a pop band, and a columnist for the alternative press since receiving her MFA from Indiana University in 1997. Now she lives and teaches in Philadelphia. Her books include *Madame Deluxe* (Coffee House Press, 2000) and *Maybe Baby* (Little, Brown, 2004).

LUANNE DIBERNARDO is a former advertising copywriter, and is the writer/producer of the feature-length film *Blowfish* and short narrative *Lemon-Lime*. She is currently working on collections of short fiction, flash fiction, a web series, and a feature-length screenplay slated for production in 2007.

CLYDE EDGERTON is the author of the novels *Lunch at the Picadilly, The Floatplane Notebooks, Raney*, and *Walking Across Egypt*.

JEAN ESTEVE lives on the Oregon coast with a couple of spanielish dogs. They all walk, swim, she writes.

BOB HICOK'S fifth book of poems is *This Clumsy Living*, published by the University of Pittsburgh Press in 2007.

NOTES ON CONTRIBUTORS

ANTHONY GOICOLEA'S work has been displayed in many galleries, including the Whitney Museum of Modern Art, the Museum of Modern Art, and the Guggenheim Museum of Art. In 2005, he was the recipient of the BMW Photo Paris Award.

KATIE ROSE GUEST lives in Greensboro, North Carolina. She earned her master's degree in creative writing from Johns Hopkins University. Her fiction and poetry have appeared in *Ellipsis, The Evansville Review, California Quarterly,* and *Connecticut River Review,* among others, and area forthcoming in *Borderlands* and *Descant.* She is currently finishing her first novel.

TONY HOAGLAND won the Poetry Foundation's 2005 Mark Twain Award for humor in American poetry. His books of poems include *What Narcissism Means to Me* (Graywolf Press, 2003) and *Donkey Gospel* (Graywolf Press, 1998). A book of craft essays, *Real Sofistikashun,* was published in October 2006 by Graywolf Press. He teaches at the University of Houston and in the Warren Wilson MFA program.

GABRIELLE JESIOLOWSKI'S poems have most recently appeared in the *Sonora Review, Cream City Review, Touchstone,* and *So to Speak.* Her manuscript, *i rose i did not dress,* was a finalist for the Slope Editions Press Book Prize. She is currently teaching, writing, and building installations out of hair and stone in Pittsburgh, Pennsylvania.

JACQUELINE KOLOSOV'S collection of poems is *Vago* (Lewis-Clark Press, 2007). Her young adult novels are *Grace from China* (Yeong & Yeong, 2004) and *The Red Queen's Daughter* (Hyperion, 2007). Recent poetry and prose appear in *Shenandoah, Passages North, Orion,* and *Windhover.* She currently directs the creative writing program at Texas Tech University. In January, she gave birth to her daughter, Sophia.

TERRY MARSHALL lives in Las Vegas where he is finishing up *Soda Springs,* a civil rights novel set in small town Colorado. He is author of *The Whole World Guide to Language Learning* (Intercultural Press, 1989), a book on how to learn unwritten languages. His short stories have appeared in two anthologies and several literary magazines.

BILL MCKIBBEN is the author of many books about global warming, alternative energy, and the risks associated with human genetic engineering. For more information on McKibben, see page fifty-four.

RICK MOODY is the author of *Demonology* (Little, Brown, 2001), *Purple America* (Little, Brown, 1997), *The Ring of Brightest Angels Around Heaven* (Little, Brown, 1995), *The Ice Storm* (Little, Brown, 1994), and *Garden State* (Pushcart Press, 2002), which won the Pushcart Press Editors' Book Award. *Right Livelihoods*, his collection of three novellas, will be published this summer by Little, Brown. Moody is a past recipient of the Addison Metcalf Award and a Guggenheim fellowship. He has contributed fiction and essays to most major publications and has been widely anthologized. He lives in New York.

EMILY MOORE is now a graduate student at the University of California Berkeley, where she studies Tlingit art of southeast Alaska. She earned a MFA in writing from West Virginia University and met the love of her life—in Alaska—the summer after this essay was written. her essays appear in *Shenandoah, Ballyhoo Stories, Phantasmagoria,* and *Oregon Quarterly.*

RAY MORRISON'S stories have appeared or are forthcoming in *Aethlon, Carve Magazine, Southern Hum,* the *Rose & Thorn,* and *moonShine review.* He lives, writes, and practices veterinary medicine in Winston-Salem, North Carolina.

WILLIAM REICHARD is the author of three collections of poetry: *This Brightness* (Mid List Press, forthcoming); *How To* (Mid List Press, 2004); and *An Alchemy in the Bones* (New Rivers Press, 1999). He's published one chapbook, *To Be Quietly Spoken* (Frith Press, 2001) and one, *Signs of Light* (META Press), is forthcoming. He is the editor of *The Evening Crowd at Kirmser's: A Gay Life in the 1940s* (University of Minnesota Press, 2001).

NOTES ON CONTRIBUTORS

RON SAVAGE has been publishing stories since age eighteen. Recent publications include *Jaberwock Review, Film Comment, G. W. Review,* and *Southern Humanities Review.* Ron has a BA and MA in psychology and a doctorate in counseling from the College of William and Mary. He has worked as an actor, a broadcaster, a newspaper editor, and for twenty-something years as psychologist senior at Eastern State Hospital in Williamsburg, Virginia. He has recently retired from everything but writing and his wife, Jan.

BRANDON R. SCHRAND teaches creative writing at the University of Idaho. His work has appeared or is forthcoming in *Tin House, Colorado Review, River Teeth, Green Mountains Review, Drunken Boat, Oklahoma Review, Isotope,* and numerous other journals. He has won the Wallace Stegner Prize and the 2006 Willard R. Espy Award, and his essay, "Collusion," was a finalist in *Drunken Boat's* Pan Literary Awards. Most recently, he was given special mention in *Pushcart Prize XXXI: Best of the Small Presses.* He just completed his memoir, *The Enders Hotel,* and he lives with his wife and two children in Moscow, Idaho.

SARAJANE WOOLF'S essays have appeared in the *Christian Science Monitor, Alaska Quarterly Review,* and *South Dakota Quarterly.* The *SDQ* piece was later named a notable essay in *Best American Essays 2004.* She lives in Carpinteria, California.

SUSAN ZAKIN is the author of *Coyotes and Town Dogs: Earth First! and the Environmental Movement* (Viking, 1993) and the editor of *Naked: Writers Uncover the Way We Live on Earth* (Four Walls Eight Windows, 2004). As a journalist, she became one of the country's most respected sources on environmental politics. She is at work on a novel about a West African warlord in exile in suburban Virginia.

MAYA JEWELL ZELLER grew up in rural Washington and Oregon. She taught high school English and coached cross-country for three years, and is currently an MFA candidate at Eastern Washington University in Spokane, where she serves as a poetry editor for *Willow Springs* and as acquisitions editor for EWU Press. Her poems have appeared in *Tidepools, Pontoon,* and *Raven Chronicles,* and are forthcoming in *Regarding Arts & Letters.*

Ecotone welcomes unsolicited works of creative nonfiction, fiction, and poetry with a specific focus on place. Submissions are accepted between August 15 and April 30 only.

Mail one prose piece and/or one to six poems at a time (mail genres separately). Prose should be typed double-spaced on one side of the page and be no longer than ten thousand words. Please query before submitting anything longer. Poems should be typed either single- or double-spaced on one side of the page. We have no preference in regards to names in headers or footers, or to staples or paper clips. Novel and memoir excerpts are acceptable if they are self-contained.

Please do not send multiple submissions in the same genre, and do not send another manuscript until you hear about the first. Include your full name and address on all envelopes. In general, address submissions to the editor in your genre. We generally follow the *Chicago Manual of Style*.

All manuscripts and correspondence regarding submissions should be accompanied by a self-addressed, stamped envelope (S.A.S.E.) for a response; no replies will be given by e-mail. Expect three months for a decision. We do not print previously published work. We do accept simultaneous submissions. We assume no responsibility for delay, loss, or damage. For more information about literary magazines, consult directories such as *NewPages*, *The Writer's Market,* and *The International Directory of Literary Magazines and Small Presses*.

Mail submissions to:
Ecotone
Genre Editor
Department of Creative Writing
University of North Carolina Wilmington
601 South College Road
Wilmington, NC 28403-3297

Ecotone does not accept electronic submissions.

Visit us online at www.uncw.edu/ecotone.

HARVARD REVIEW

Harvard Review publishes poetry, fiction, essays, drama, graphics, and reviews. It is published twice yearly, in spring and autumn, and is available by subscription and from select bookstores.

Visit us online at
hcl.harvard.edu/ harvardreview

BEST AMERICAN POETRY 2002, 2006
BEST AMERICAN SHORT STORIES 2003, 2005
BEST AMERICAN ESSAYS 2003, 2004
BEST AMERICAN MYSTERY STORIES 2006
PUSHCART PRIZE 2001, 2004

HARVARD REVIEW
Lamont Library
Harvard University,
Cambridge, MA 02138
Ph: 617-495-9775
Fax: 617-496-3692

FALL 2006

ALICE HOFFMAN &
ALAN HEATHCOCK

LYDIA DAVIS &
TONY HORWITZ

MARILYN CHIN &
BRENDAN GALVIN

SPRING 2006

KATHERINE VAZ &
ANTHONY VARALLO

BLAKE BAILEY &
MELVIN BUKIET

TOMAZ SALAMUN
& GEORGE SEFERIS

SUMMER 2006

GORE VIDAL &
KAREN BENDER

DRAMA
THERESA REBECK

DENISE DUHAMEL,
COLE SWENSEN &
LAURIE SHECK

SUMMER 2006

JOYCE CAROL OATES
& JIM CRACE

SAMUEL MENASHE

MARIO VARGAS LLOSA
& MARION HALLIGAN

Western State College of Colorado's

*M*arginalia
literary magazine

Publishes yearly in the fall
Issues available for $9 each
Accepts online submissions only
Reads all year
Sponsors an annual college prose contest

At Marginalia, we are interested in the interplay between the contained text and its surrounding negative space. For this reason, we encourage work that demonstrates mastery of any given genre, as well as work that transgresses or blurs established forms.

Authors we've published:
Mary Crow,
Brian Evenson,
R.S. Gwynn,
Laird Hunt,
Mark Irwin,
Steve Katz,
Gina Ochsner,
George Saunders,
George Singleton,
Wendy Walker

Complete submissions and contest guidelines, and sample work available at
www.western.edu/marginalia

MFA in Fiction Poetry Creative Nonfiction

JOIN US in one of the **few independent creative writing departments** in the nation and study writing in workshops, craft seminars, and individual conferences with our distinguished faculty. Participate in **The Publishing Laboratory**, a fully functioning micropress, or work on *Ecotone*, our national literary magazine of environmental writing. All within a welcoming coastal community rich in culture, natural history, heritage, and support for the arts.

Teaching assistantships, fellowships, and scholarships are available.

Faculty Lavonne Adams, Tim Bass, Barbara Brannon, Wendy Brenner, Mark Cox, Clyde Edgerton, Philip Furia, Philip Gerard, David Gessner, Rebecca Lee, Sarah Messer, Malena Mörling, Robert Siegel, Michael White

Visiting Faculty Recent guests include Rick Bass, Richard Bausch, Robert Creeley, Mark Doty, Allan Gurganus, Brenda Hillman, Randall Kenan, Philip Levine, Alison Lurie, Jill McCorkle, Heather McHugh, Donna Tartt, Terry Tempest Williams

910.962.3070 • mfa@uncw.edu
www.uncw.edu/writers

University of North Carolina **Wilmington**
Department of Creative Writing
601 South College Road, Wilmington NC 28403-5938
UNCW is an EEO/AA institution.

Innovative programs for writers on the Carolina Coast

Ecotone
reimagining place

Subscriptions:
Back issues: $5
One-year (two issues): $15
Two-years (four issues): $25
Three-years (six issues): $35

❏ send me a ____ -year subscription for $____.

Name: _____
Address: _____
_____
Phone number: _____
E-mail address: _____

Mail check payable to UNCW Creative Writing Department, subject line *Ecotone* subscription, and mail to :

Ecotone
Department of Creative Writing
University of North Carolina Wilmington
601 South College Road
Wilmington, NC 28403-3297

Ecotone
reimagining place

Volume 1, Number 1
Winter/Spring 2005

featuring the work of *Mark Doty, Clyde Edgerton, Alicia Erian, Brad Land, Philip Levine, Bill Roorbach, Reg Saner, and Ann Zwinger.*

Volume 1, Number 2
Winter/Spring 2006

featuring the work of *Ann Darby, Barbara Fisher, Sheila Kohler, Sebastian Matthews, David Rivard, Jennifer Sinor, and Mike White*

Volume 2, Number 1
Fall/Winter 2006

featuring the work of *Julianna Baggott, Rebecca Barry, Aimee Bender, Jill McCorkle, Lia Purpura, Reg Saner, and Joan Snyder.*